Black and White Justice in Little Dixie

Three Historical Essays

Doug Hunt

"A Course in Applied Lynching" was first published in a slightly different form in the *Missouri Review*, Volume 27, Number 2, 2004, and was printed as a separate short book entitled *Summary Justice* in 2010.

The photograph of Stewart Bridge on the cover and on page 34 is from the Western Historical Manuscript Collection, Columbia (Arnot M. Finley Photograph Albums) and is used by permission.

For my daughter and her generation, who may do better

Contents

Preface

The essays collected here describe events in Columbia, Missouri, a community that might be a microcosm of the United States in general. It is a Midwestern city with Southern roots and a population attracted from elsewhere and everywhere by the presence of a large university and two colleges.

In its early years Columbia was the principal city of Little Dixie, a cluster of counties along the Missouri River dominated by slave-holding families. Anyone who reads the city's history or even watches the local news quickly realizes that race has continued to be a source of tension in Columbia, but in this respect it may not be much different from the dozens of other Columbias scattered from Maine to California.

The three essays describe events separated by intervals of about 90 years. Some Columbians alive when the slave Sanford sued for his freedom were still living when James Scott was lynched. Some Columbians born before the Scott lynching lived long enough to read about the arrest of Mercury Merrick in their newspapers and, if they were so inclined, to view the video on YouTube.

Together, the essays remind us that in America, no generation starts fresh when it comes to race relations. We have a past to understand and live with.

$100 REWARD:

R AN AWAY from the subscriber, living in Boone county, Mo. on Friday the 13th June,

THREE NEGROES,

viz DAVE, and JUDY his wife; and JOHN, their son. Dave is about 32 years of age, light color for a full blooded negro—is a good boot and shoe maker by trade: is also a good farm hand. He is about 5 feet 10 or 11 inches high, stout made, and quite an artful, sensible fellow. Had on when he went away, coat and pantaloons of brown woollen jeans, shirt of home made flax linen, and a pair of welted shoes. Judy is rather slender made, about 28 years old, has a very light complexion for a negro; had on a dress made of flax linen, striped with copperas and blue; is a first rate house servant and seamstress, and a good spinner, and is very full of affectation when spoken to. John is 9 years old, very likely and well grown; is remarkably light colored for a negro, and is cross-eyed. Had on a pair of brown jeans pantaloons, bleached flax linen shirt, and red flannel one under it, and a new straw hat.

I will give the above reward and all reasonable expenses, if secured any where out of the State, so that I can get them again, or $50 if taken within the State—$30 for Dave alone, and $20 for Judy and John, and the same in proportion out of the state. The above mentioned clothing was all they took with them from home, but it is supposed he had $30 or $40 in cash with him, so that he may buy and exchange their clothing.

WILLIAM LIENTZ.

Boone county, Mo. June 17, 1834:   52-2

8

Names

Oh, Justice, when expelled from other habitations, make
this thy dwelling place.

—Inscription at the courthouse door,
Boone County, Missouri

In the decades before emancipation, thousands of
slaves lived within walking distance of the courthouse in
Columbia, Missouri. Most of their names and stories are
lost forever. They appear on census records and tax rolls as
tally marks or digits. Their marriages had no meaning under
state law, and so were not registered. Their births, deaths,
and burials were unrecorded, even in the family bibles of
their owners. In wills and estate documents we find a few
names and sometimes cash values, but little else.

Hard work by genealogists and historians may
eventually connect a few hundred slaves' names to
particular acts or events. In 1829 "Dinah, a woman of color"
joined the Columbia Presbyterian Church along with her
owners, making her one of the first twenty-five members. In
1840 a slave named Armstead was permitted to "go at large
upon a hiring of his own time, and to act and deal as a free
person," an offense against Missouri's slave code that cost
his master a twenty-dollar fine. In 1850, "Henry, a slave"

was given thirty lashes for keeping a shotgun in his house on a farm north of town. Dinah, Armstead, and Henry: everything we know about them can be squeezed into a single sentence.

We can learn a little more about a few slaves connected with prominent families. In 1859, a boy named Jimmie was born in the manor house of Judge David Gordon. He was born, in fact, in the bedroom of his mistress, Hulda Gordon. Jimmie's father was the family's yardman and his mother the maid. They lived with several other slaves in the original Gordon family log cabin, which was just a few steps from the manor house. After he learned to walk, Jimmie followed his mother while she did her work. Eventually the mistress, "Miss Hulda," began to assign him simple chores. "I was a quick rascal," he recalled years later, "and I thought the faster I did a thing the better."

> She always had me sweep down the staircase in the front hall. One day she stood at the top of the stairs and watched me zip down them. Then she said, 'Come up here, Jimmie.' She stepped to a closet and pulled out a red toy broom.
> 'Now, Jimmie,' she said, 'Take this one and let me tell you how to sweep those steps. See that dust back between the banisters?'
> 'Yes'm,' I replied.
> 'That's right, Jimmie, boy. Reach way back and get every speck of it!'
> So I swept down those steps with her watching me. When I got to the bottom, I had twice as much dirt as I had the first time. And that's the way Miss Hulda taught me that it wasn't speed, but thoroughness, that makes a job well done.

Jimmie soon learned that outside the circle of his mistress's kindness, slavery could be harsh. Some owners disciplined their slaves by sending them to the slave breaker:

> He was a big, brawny man, and he was mean. He had a place here in town—I guess it was about where Clink-scales garage is now—and whenever a slave became too unruly, his master took him in to the slave breaker, who didn't often fail to beat the rebellion out of him. The slave breaker had a pen with a log fence about ten or twelve feet high. He'd put the 'bad Nigger' in there and beat him several times a day.

Jimmie's master, David Gordon, had a more gentlemanly way of dealing with recalcitrant slaves. "Whenever he couldn't do anything with one, he'd call him in and say, 'I'm sorry, Dick, but I'm going to have to ship you south.' And then he'd send him off with the next slave trader who came through town."

James Williams was seventy years old when he told these stories, and had been a successful business owner for forty years. He was neatly dressed in a dark suit and tie, and was being interviewed in the living room of the old Gordon cabin, which was being refurbished as a clubhouse for the women of Stephens College. The journalist who interviewed him tells us that everyone in town called him "Uncle Jim."

IT SEEMS to have been almost instinctive for Columbia's slaveholders to contrast the life of blacks in their town with the life of blacks "down South." Everyone seemed to agree that *down there* slavery was an inhumane institution. *Up here* things were better. Slaves were generally well-fed and well-clothed. If they were sick, they were cared for by the same doctors their masters were. If they were churchgoers, they attended the same church. Tobacco and cotton weren't major crops in the area, so very few slaves in Boone County labored in gangs under the supervision of a hired overseer. Typically, they did the same kinds of physical work free white people did, and often they worked side-by-side with their owners or their owner's children.

An 1834 advertisement from Columbia's newspaper, the *Intelligencer*, includes a thumbnail sketch of a slave family, written by their owner, William Lientz.

$100 REWARD:

Ran away from the subscriber, living in Boone county, Mo. on Friday the 13th June,

THREE NEGROES,

viz: **DAVE**, and **JUDY**, his wife; and **JOHN**, their son. Dave is about 32 years of age, light colored for a full blooded negro—is a very good boot and shoe maker by trade: is also a good farm hand. He is about 5 feet 10 or 11 inches high, stout made, and quite an artful, sensible fellow. Had on when he went away, coat and pantaloons of brown woolen jeans, shirt of home made flax linen, and a pair of welted shoes: Judy is rather slender made, about 28 years old, has a very light complexion for a negro; had on a dress made of flax linen, striped with copperas and blue; is a first rate house servant and seamstress, and a good spinner, and is very full of affectation when spoken to. John is 9 years old, very likely and well grown; is remarkably light colored for a negro, and is cross-eyed. Had on a pair of brown jeans pantaloons, bleached flax linen shirt, and red flannel one under it, and a new straw hat.

As slaves of one of the richest men in the area, this family was better off materially than many poor whites. Dave may have "$30 or $40 of cash with him," the advertisement goes on to say, and it doesn't accuse him of having stolen the money. Owners in the area generally gave their slaves evenings off and a long Sabbath—Saturday afternoon to Monday morning. By local custom (and despite state law) they could keep for themselves what they earned during this free time.

And yet Dave, Judy, and John were running away, and risking a good deal by doing so, since any white man who captured them might sell them down South. What compelled them to take the chance? Lientz's elaborate description of skin colors could suggest that John's biological father was white, but the three slaves fled together, as a family. The records we can find tell us that the great motive of runaways in the Columbia area was not an abstract longing for freedom, or even a fear of brutality or sexual abuse. It was fear that husbands would be sold away from wives, wives from husbands, or children from parents. This wasn't a groundless fear. The selling of children about John's age was commonplace. In the natural course of things, white children married and moved away. Black children had to be sold or given away if they weren't to accumulate indefinitely, and they were especially marketable after they were old enough to do light chores, but before they became teenagers.

Slaves ran away often enough for the publisher of the *Intelligencer*, Nathaniel Patten, to earn a steady trickle of income by printing advertisements for their recapture. He laid out the ads beautifully, sometimes decorating them with icons of slaves. The ad for the recapture of Dave, Judy, and John includes images of a black man and a black woman fleeing, one left, one right, each carrying a small bundle. Patten profited from these ads and others for slave auctions and hirings, and he owned one or two slaves who helped him in the print shop and the house. Nonetheless, he looked forward hopefully to the day when society would be "freed from so lamentable an evil as slavery." In April of 1835 he ran a story that reminded his readers of its human cost.

> **SUICIDE**—A negro man, named Michael (a slave) committed suicide in the jail of this county, on Tuesday night last, by hanging himself.
> The circumstances which led to this melancholy act were, we learn, as follows. He was recently sold, by a Mr. Barnett, of Howard county, to Mr. J. E. Fenton, of this county, by whom he was immediately shipped for the *South*. At the mouth of the Ohio, he contrived, by filing off his irons, to make his escape, and returned to this county, or Howard, where his wife resides. He refused to be sent to the South unless his wife should also accompany him: and being armed, would not surrender himself but upon this condition. He was, however, by a stratagem, finally taken, and placed, for safe keeping, in our jail—where finding that he was about to be sent away without his wife, and that he would in all probability never see her again, he resolved to end both his life and his servitude.

MISSOURI, FOLLOWING the model of Virginia and Kentucky, granted slaves a slender bill of rights. Slaves accused of serious crimes had the right to counsel and to trial by jury. It was a crime for anyone, masters included, to deprive them of life or limb or treat them inhumanely. On Sundays, they could not be required to work except in "ordinary household offices of daily necessity or charity."

14

How slaves actually fared under the law generally depended on the character of the local Justice of the Peace. Justices didn't keep official records, so we will never have a full picture of how energetic they were in protecting the rights of slaves. The anecdotes are discouraging. Once a small iron safe was stolen from a store in Columbia, and suspicion fell on four slaves. The Justice before whom they appeared found no evidence against them, but ordered twenty lashes each anyway and, for good measure, ordered their master to "sell them down South."

The standard of justice was higher in the Circuit Court, but slaves seldom appeared there unless they were accused of serious crimes. Few had enough money to hire lawyers. They couldn't testify in their own behalf. They had no right to sue. The door of the courthouse was locked against them. But Missouri's statutes provided them one way of knocking at it. If they had evidence that they were *illegally* enslaved, and if they could find a lawyer willing to represent them, they could petition for the right to sue *as if* they were free. In 1833, Judge David Todd heard such a knock and answered it.

Judge Todd had presided over the Boone County Circuit Court since its inception, assisted by his brother Roger North Todd, who was the Court's Clerk and sometimes its straight man. In April of 1821, at the opening session, there was no courthouse and hardly any town. The Todds sat in a maple grove. When the session opened, Todd put on the whole dignity of his office, referring to himself in third person, as "the Court," and addressing his brother formally as "Mr. Clerk." Their first case involved a farmer accused of defrauding the state by cutting a single wolf scalp in halves in order to collect two bounties. The Court fined the scalper $5 and costs and ordered Mr. Clerk to enter the judgment. Justice had arrived.

The Todds were the Missouri branch of a prominent Kentucky family. Abraham Lincoln, who married their niece, sometimes said, "God himself finds one *d* adequate for His name, but the Todds need two." David, who came west owning twenty slaves, might have set up in Missouri as a prosperous merchant or planter, or plunged directly into politics. Instead, he fastened himself to the First Judicial Circuit, which in the earliest days had a population of a few thousand spread over a land area the size of Switzerland. Nearly half his days were spent away from home, and his salary didn't reliably cover the expenses of his large family. He was chronically short on cash. Boone County creditors sued him in his own courtroom. "It has been discovered that the defendant is the judge of this court," he would announce, deadpan, before sending the case to another judicial circuit. Or he would say to his brother, "Mr. Clerk, enter a judgment against David Todd by default."

On law days, he opened court at nine in the morning, adjourned at noon, and napped before returning for a session that might run late into the evening. One afternoon while a lawyer made a long argument to the jury, he nodded off in his chair. When he snapped awake, he interrupted the argument to call to his brother, "Mr. Clerk, enter up a fine of ten dollars against David Todd for contempt of court. I'll break up this habit of going to sleep or I'll break the Court." Another day a stonemason named Campbell, who had watched a morning argument about ownership of a horse, returned to the courthouse after the noon recess, stumbled, and fell to the floor. When Todd asked what was wrong, Campbell replied, "Judge, I am a horse. I am a horse, Judge." He was obviously drunk. Even the Court may have smiled: "Mr. Sheriff," Todd said, "take this horse out and lock him in my stable and keep him there until I call for him." It was probably Todd's personality as much as his sharp mind that made him a successful judge. People trusted him because they instinctively liked him and liked him because they instinctively trusted him.

ON JULY 17, 1833, a young man named Sanford (or "Sant") came to Judge Todd to complain that he was held illegally in slavery by a man named Mark Reavis. Todd couldn't have been taken entirely by surprise. Almost exactly a year before, Sanford's father, Philip Shirkey, had filed suits in Saline County, attempting to free four children held in slavery there by Solomon Reavis, Mark's brother.

When Solomon Reavis learned that the suits had been filed, he had assembled Shirkey's children and told them that they should go to their father's house. They would be allowed to stay permanently with their parents, he told them, "if they saw fit." They never arrived. Solomon Reavis, fearing that he would lose the lawsuit and the slaves, had sold them secretly to a man named Michael Castly. Castly and his accomplices had waylaid the children en route and taken them to parts unknown—to Texas, it was rumored. Philip Shirkey and his wife Patience had been fighting frantically to recover their children ever since.

Legally, Philip and Patience Shirkey were "free persons of color." Though they were poor and illiterate, they kept Solomon Reavis constantly in court and peppered him through their attorney with interrogatories about the children's whereabouts. They had advertisements inserted in the *Arkansas Gazette* and perhaps in other Southern newspapers:

STOP THE KIDNAPPERS

Notice to all whom it may concern:

On or about the first of August (inst.) were forcibly **KIDNAPPED**, in the county of Saline, in the State of Missouri, **FOUR CHILDREN**, of red or mulatto color, free persons — one, a male, about 15 years old, and three females, the oldest about 13, and the others about 2 and 4 years younger, brother an sisters, and children of a free woman of color by the name of PATIENCE. These children and their mother once belonged to one Isham Reavis, in his life time, who died in said county of Saline; and it is believed that one COSTELLO and others have taken said children into Arkansas Territory, or south of that, to sell and enslave them. The names of the children are Shelby, or Shelny, Julia, Timy, and Eliza.

It is to be hoped that all GOOD citizens will use their best exertions to detect the villain or villains, and forward any information they may be able to gain in relation to said unfortunate children, or their brutal kidnappers, to the undersigned, directed to the Post Office at Boonville, Missouri, as soon as may be.

Philip Shirkey
Boonville, Mo. August 2, 1832

What Judge Todd was facing was an overflow into Boone County of the struggle between the white Reavis clan and the black Shirkey clan.

Sanford was the sibling, about 21 years old, of the kidnapped children. Peyton Hayden, who had prepared their legal cases, had also prepared the petition Sanford brought with him now. "Your petitioner a person of colour respect-fully sheweth …," the petition began. In the starched legal language that attorney Hayden managed well, the illiterate "person of colour" shewed that

> ➢ His mother was Patience, for many years a slave of Isham Reavis.

> ➢ For two years, about 1809-10, Isham Reavis moved his household from Kentucky into Illinois, then part of the Northwestern Territory, and Patience lived there with him as his slave.

There, to the Judge's expert eye, was a crucial fact. Under the U. S. law, the Northwestern Territory had been free soil, and any slave who resided there became a free person. Isham and Patience may both have believed at the time that she remained his slave, but if they did, they were both legally wrong.

> ➢ Later, Isham and his household returned to Kentucky, where Sanford was born, and where both he and his mother were kept for years as slaves.

By law, a child born of a free woman was free. And so it seemed that Sanford, whose mixture of black and white ancestry showed clearly in his face, was no more a slave than David Todd's own children were. Judge Todd was one of the largest slaveholders in Columbia, but he had announced from the bench that blacks, even slaves, had rights that every free man was "bound to respect." Hayden's petition erected a ladder of legal logic, and the judge climbed it dutifully.

> ➢ After Isham Reavis came to Missouri, he sold Sanford to Edmund Reavis, who sold him in turn to Mark Reavis.

> ➢ Mark Reavis "well knows that your petitioner is a free person—yet he holds your petitioner in bondage as a slave."

Peyton Hayden's petition didn't mention the possibility that Reavis honestly misunderstood Sanford's legal status, though such a mistake would have been basis enough for the lawsuit. The lawyer was firing a warning shot over Mark Reavis's head. *Deliberately* holding a free person in bondage was a serious offense in Missouri. In a civil trial, it could force the defendant to pay "smart money" compensating the plaintiff for years of unpaid labor. In a criminal trial, it could lead to hanging.

JUDGE TODD had known Peyton Hayden for many years. Both had been early settlers in Franklin, a pioneer town that had vanished under the waters of the shifting Missouri River. There had been oversupply of lawyers in Franklin then, and Hayden—who had arrived with no fortune except his education—had been unable for some time to find clients. In a frontier town notable for masculine swagger, his appearance may have worked against him. He was petite and clean-shaven, and he wore his hair in the long braid favored by Southerners of an earlier generation. At first glance he might have been mistaken for a woman.

Without clients, he turned briefly to teaching school. Kit Carson was one of his pupils, which can't have been a happy experience for either of them. In 1819, through the good offices of an established lawyer, he finally landed a client. Successes in court gradually enlarged his practice, and now he rode Judge Todd's circuit regularly, representing clients in several counties.

Names

Long acquaintance and mutual respect had made the judge and the lawyer friends. According to a favorite courthouse story, they were riding the circuit together once and stopped in the evening at a boardinghouse. The landlady met them at the door and gave Hayden a stern looking over. Other lawyers, it seems, had whispered to her that Judge Todd was traveling with a woman who was no better than she should be. The landlady's inspection of Hayden seemed to confirm the story. She told Todd that she had a room for him, but that the "old hussy" would have to go elsewhere. Todd tried to explain that Hayden was a lawyer and a friend, and that they would gladly share a room. "Yes," the landlady answered, "I suppose she is your friend; maybe my husband has friends like that, but he never brought any of them into my house."

Hayden had crafted a compelling petition for Sanford. To show that Patience had lived on free soil in Illinois, he attached a notarized statement from an unassailable source—Sally Reavis, Mark's stepmother and Isham's widow, who had lived there with her. The same statement gave the firmest possible evidence that Sanford was Patience's child: Sally Reavis had been the midwife at the birthing. If Mark Reavis wanted to dispute the central facts, he would have to contradict his stepmother and other white relatives Hayden had lined up as witnesses.

Sanford sued not only for freedom, but for civil damages. If the case went to trial, the jury would hear testimony about Reavis's worst behavior, when he

> with force and arms made an assault upon the said Sanford … seized and laid hold of the said Sanford … pulled and dragged about him the said Sanford, and …

> struck him the said Sanford a great many violent blows
> and stokes ... and kept and detained him the said San-
> ford in prison ... for a space of six months ... against
> the will of the said Sanford....

For these injuries, Hayden asked on behalf of his client monetary damages of $500.

Hayden had crafted equally skillful petitions for San-ford's siblings, however, and was painfully aware of the results. Word had reached him that Reavis intended to sell Sanford—might in fact already have sold him—to a slave trader named Edward Camplin, who planned, in turn, to sell him down South. Hayden informed Todd of this rumor, and asked the Court to protect his client. He wanted Reavis to be ordered not to take Sanford outside the jurisdiction of the court, and he wanted him ordered to give Sanford "reasonable liberty" to meet with his lawyer. But since such orders hadn't adequately protected Shelby, Julia, Timy, and Eliza, he wanted more. He wanted Mark Reavis to post a substantial bond *guaranteeing* Sanford's appearance in court.

The Court understood. Todd had Sanford swear to the truthfulness of facts in the petition and then sign it with his mark. Then Todd instructed his brother to draw up a writ of habeas corpus commanding Reavis to bring Sanford to the Judge's house in Columbia to "hear and abide" the steps by which the Court would protect the young man from abduction. "Herein fail not at your peril, or show cause why you do not obey the command of this writ."

When Mark Reavis received the papers, he hired a lawyer, who drafted a careful response:

> Before the suing out of the said writ, the said Sanford
> absconded from my possession and hath privately
> avoided and prevented me from regaining him, and

hath ever since, and doth still, keep himself out of my power to produce him.

This might actually have been true. Sanford had every reason to avoid Reavis if he could. Still, the Court was skeptical. On August 7, Todd sent the sheriff out with a second writ demanding that Reavis bring Sanford immediately to the courthouse. This one worked. Reavis brought Sanford to the Judge and posted a $500 recognizance bond.

MARK REAVIS had already had unpleasant dealings with the Court. He had arrived in Boone County a decade earlier, bought a farm ten miles west of town, and immediately been sued for nonpayment of a debt. He had incurred the debt by buying—on credit—a slave named Oney and her three young children. The creditor could produce the bill of sale, so Judge Todd had ordered Reavis to pay.

Reavis had consulted a lawyer and counter-sued, saying that he was the innocent victim in the case. Oney was afflicted with "the white swelling" (tuberculosis of the bone), and Reavis claimed that his creditor had concealed the defect. She was so lame that she was "of but little use or service." Reading the court record reminds us that neither buyers nor sellers of slaves were likely to be angels. In the end, Judge Todd had found for the creditor. He had commanded Reavis to pay up, with 6% interest, plus court costs. Whatever lesson Reavis took away from this incident he had purchased dearly.

On the whole, the Reavis clan were not sophisticates. They were backwoodsmen. The men often lived to the age of biblical patriarchs, and they preferred to keep children and grandchildren near them, under their patriarchal authority. Isham Reavis, Mark's father, was part of a colony of Reavises that had swarmed from Kentucky about 1817. Many of them settled near a salt pond in a remote region of Saline County. Isham was the designated preacher for the Salt Pond Reavises, so he may have been literate enough to read his bible, but his wife Sally never learned to sign her name.

Isham's will, written in 1824, shows that he was better pleased with some of his sons than with others. Edward and Solomon, who had kept to the Salt Pond area, were given sums of cash. Charles, who had not, was emphatically disowned. William, whose failings we can't guess, was "hire[d] to his brother Edward for two years, for somewhere about $129." Mark was not mentioned by name. Perhaps he had displeased his father by taking his family across the river to Boone County.

Mark was fifty-one years old when he made this move, and several of his children and grandchildren moved with him. One of the sons—close to Sanford in age—was Doctor Reavis, who was never a doctor. Mark had apparently named him for the physician who delivered him.

The Reavis colony in Boone County stayed intact and intermarried repeatedly with their near neighbors, the Berrys. Except when he was forced into the courtroom Mark Reavis seemed to have had little interest in Columbia, and Columbia had little interest in him. His name appeared in the *Intelligencer* just four times in ten years: once because he had found a stray horse, three times because he had uncollected letters waiting at the post office. The census taker of 1830 guessed that his last name was "Rivis," and no one corrected the spelling. Nothing we know about Mark

Reavis or his children suggests that they understood much about the world beyond their immediate neighborhood, or wanted to.

Sixty-one now, Reavis can't have looked forward to dealing with the Court again. A Reavis family story says that a lawyer advised him to sell Sanford quickly, before the case went to trial. It was a bad situation any way a person looked at it, but if he could unload the slave before the Court emancipated him, the sale would net a few hundred dollars even after the recognizance bond was paid. And if it could be made to seem that Sanford had vanished on his own volition, even the bond might be saved. It was worth thinking about.

AT THE next session of the Circuit Court, Reavis asked through his lawyer that the case be continued until February, a routine request that was granted on October 28.

By mid-November, Reavis and Ned Camplin had settled on a sales price of $1200, with Sanford to be delivered under cover of darkness to a waiting steamboat at the Brady landing on the Terrapin Neck. Reavis sent his son James and two other men (Thomas Berry and Joel Hern) into the slave house about nightfall on November 16. The men forced Sanford's head into a noose and dragged him, choking, out the door. They threw him on a horse, strapped him down, and started for the river.

It was a fine night for an abduction: unseasonably warm and cloudless, with a crescent moon nearing the western horizon. Before the men reached the Terrapin Neck, the moon had set. Apparently they paused for a time within sight of the river, waiting to make their rendezvous. While they waited, the earth entered the tail of the comet that would eventually be named Tempel-Tuttle.

In Boston citizens rushed from their houses to see meteors filling the sky densely enough to make one reporter compare them to snowflakes. A civil engineer in New York estimated that 10,000 were falling per hour. In rural Virginia, a preacher heard one of his children shout, "Come to the door, father, the world is surely coming to an end" Another child shouted, "See! The whole heavens are on fire! All the stars are falling!" Across the eastern half of the continent, hardened sinners were rattled: gamblers threw their cards in the fire and at least one sailor swore that he would stop swearing.

In Salem, Illinois, Abraham Lincoln was wakened by knocking at his door. It was the Presbyterian deacon with whom he was boarding: "Arise, Abraham, the day of judgment has come!" Lincoln sprang to the window and saw the sky filled with falling stars, but he knew enough astronomy to recognize that behind the meteors, the familiar constellations had stayed in place. Joseph Smith, fleeing murderous anti-Mormon mobs in Jackson County, Missouri, watched the tails of the meteors "curl and twist up like serpents writhing."

David Todd and his wife were out of town the night of the meteor shower, enjoying a working vacation by riding a segment of the judge's circuit together. They took the younger children with them, but left the older ones in the charge of Mrs. Patten, wife of the newspaper editor. Anne, the oldest daughter, remembered sixty years later that she

> ...was wakened by Mrs. Patten calling me to get up
> and behold the heavens in a blaze of glory. The firma-

ment was illumined brighter than by sunlight and the starry host seemed to have contributed to a brilliant shower of spangles that fell more as snowflakes fall than like direct drops of a pouring rain. I remember holding my apron to catch them after the surprise wore away, for they were shining not burning lights. Mrs. Patten had been aroused by the shouts and cries of the negroes of our neighbors and the singing and praying of our own servants whose spirit of excitement and superstition we young members of the family imbibed, and I must confess for a while we actually expected to hear Gabriel's trumpet and see the dead arise.

Someone rang the bell at Gentry's tavern, and someone else the bell of the Presbyterian Church. Citizens poured onto streets, able to see one another plainly, though the peculiarly white light had drained all the color from their faces.

William Switzler, later a prominent lawyer and historian, was a teenager in 1833. Older men in a position to know later told him what happened on the Terrapin Neck that night. In the predawn hours, the kidnappers stayed back in the woods and listened for "the wheezing of the engines or the rattle of the paddle wheels" that would tell them that the steamboat was coming into the landing. When they heard it, they brought Sanford down to the riverside in manacles.

Of a sudden, the earth, sky, and even the river, seemed afire. They looked up to see stars falling from their places...not one, two or a half dozen, but by thousands. The woods were a sheet of fire, while Camplin's steamboat stood midstream in a shower of hissing flame. The hills beyond loomed ghost-like in the supernatural light.

Sanford fell to his knees and began to pray. "The white men were good farmers," according to Switzler, "but their astronomical education had been neglected." They believed that they were witnessing the dawn of Judgment Day. Christ would soon come to judge the quick and the dead, and "they were determined not to be caught redhanded." They freed Sanford and all went their separate ways. "It was not until the next day," Switzler says, "when they found the earth and sky still intact and that the stars had not fallen, that the white men told the story about which their friends never ceased to twit them."

NORTH TODD Gentry, grandson of the court Clerk, says that "newspaper men from far and near" were present the day the trial began. Ordinary citizens would have been there, too. It was the end of February, a slack season for farmers, and a time when townspeople were tired of being confined to their houses. Arguments in the courthouse were generally better entertainment than arguments at home. A win for Reavis would be reassuring to Columbians for whom the subordination of blacks to whites seemed a part of the natural order or things. A win for Sanford would unsettle them. It would be a reminder that the forces that held together the slave system were not as immutable as those that held together the solar system.

Spectators had reason to anticipate a better-than-average legal show. Despite his short stature, Peyton Hayden was a dramatic presence in the courtroom, and Reavis was represented by three lawyers with star power—a sitting state representative, a future justice of the state Supreme Court, and a future governor. The jurors were neighbors and friends of the spectators, drawn from every corner of the county. Some were slaveholders; some were

not. Some in the gallery would have heard rumors of Sanford's miraculous escape on the night the stars fell, which
must have added to their curiosity.

They may have found the trial disappointingly short.
The November abduction was not directly relevant to the
case filed back in July, so testimony about it was presuma-
bly disallowed. There was no ambiguity about the central
facts. With Reavis's own stepmother testifying for the
prosecution, not even the most ingenious defense lawyer
could argue that Patience had never lived in Illinois or that
Sanford was not Patience's child. Before the jurors went out
to deliberate, Judge Todd gave them narrow instructions: if
the testimony showed that Patience "was taken into the
Northwestern Territory ... then Patience by such residence
became free." If the testimony convinced jurors that Sanford was Patience's son, born after her residence on free
soil, "then he is free also, and ... the Jury ought to find a
verdict accordingly." Having been told what their plain duty
was, the jurors did it quickly. They declared that "Sanford, a
man of color" should have his freedom and be awarded
$100 in damages.

The week after the verdict, Sanford and Hayden
pressed their advantage. They started a fresh civil lawsuit,
this one for assault on November 16. If Hayden could convince a jury that Reavis had engineered that attack because
he knew Sanford was rightfully a free man, the monetary
damages could be ruinous. On the same day, the Court
issued summonses to Reavis and his accomplices. They
were to appear in the June term to answer charges of
contempt for attempting to remove Sanford from the
Court's jurisdiction. Sanford would, naturally, be the star

witness in the contempt case, and out of his testimony might come other criminal charges—even the capital charge of knowingly holding a free person as a slave.

Reavis was in serious danger, but so was Sanford. Reavis's attorneys had quickly appealed the jury's finding to the Missouri Supreme Court, claiming an error in Judge Todd's instructions. The effect was to freeze Sanford in slavery. Until every avenue of appeal was exhausted—an indefinite length of time, with many opportunities for delay—Sanford would remain Reavis's property and Reavis would have a right to control his movements. The events of the last two years, both north and south of the river, had shown that no court could protect a black person in the custody of the Reavis family.

Mark Reavis had every reason to want Sanford to vanish, and within three months, Sanford did. His court appearance in early March is the last clearly documented moment of his life. When the Circuit Court reconvened in June, his civil case, which would have required the participation of a living plaintiff, was dismissed. The trail of contemporary documents goes cold here, and we are compelled to imagine the worst—that sometime in the spring of 1834, Sanford was abducted or killed.

IF WE want to consider an alternative ending, we can begin with this statement William Switzler made to a reporter in 1904:

> What became of the negro? The next heard of him he was with Marney and Hicks in the first of the expeditions over the old Santa Fe trail and the last known of him he had married a Mexican woman and was the richest mulatto in the whole Southwest.

At first blush, the story seems unlikely—a fairy tale spun out by an old man known for putting a positive face on some of the dark episodes of Columbia history. On closer examination, however, it grows more plausible.

Almost immediately after the jury returned its verdict on February 27, Mark Reavis and his son James left Boone County—where they had been publicly villainized—and went to the Salt Pond area to live nearer the ancestral hive. We know this from a subpoena that chased them. Mark left his Boone County legal problems in the hands of sons who hadn't participated in the November abduction. This we know from court records and a power of attorney he signed February 28. It was with Anderson Reavis (age 31) and perhaps with Doctor Reavis (age 25) that Peyton Hayden and the Court now dealt.

On March 6 Hayden was wary enough of the Reavises' intentions to ask Judge Todd for an additional bond insuring that Sanford would be kept safe and not be taken outside the jurisdiction of the court. By March 11, something had changed: Hayden withdrew the request for the bond. Apparently the parties were beginning to find common ground. It was in no one's interest, really, for Sanford to remain in the area, threatening Mark Reavis in court and being threatened by him out of court. It was in no one's interest, really, for him to be removed from the area by a crime, with the attendant risk of prosecution.

Amos Marney and Young E. Hicks were in Columbia that spring, organizing a Santa Fe caravan that would leave in May. It wasn't, as Switzler said, "the first of the expeditions." The trade had been going on for a decade, and there were several men in Columbia who could explain to

Sanford—and to Philip and Patience Shirkey, his distraught parents—that Santa Fe was a prosperous town filled with dark-skinned people whose freedom was not in doubt or danger.

They could also explain to the Reavis brothers that the town was in a foreign country, 1200 miles away, on the other side of an inhospitable desert occupied by hostile Indians, so that the chance of Sanford's returning to the courthouse in Columbia was negligible. Mark Reavis had already been assessed $100 in damages by the jury, and he had just signed another $250 bond, payable to Sanford, as a condition of filing the appeal. When the appeal failed, which it certainly would, he would owe Sanford $350 plus costs. Wouldn't it be in everyone's best interest for the Reavises to give Sanford at least part of the money to pay his passage and start him on a new life?

Is there any way to confirm that a deal was struck and that Sanford reached the Southwest and married that Mexican woman? The question forces us against problems familiar to every African-American genealogist. In the transition between slavery and freedom, names changed. Freedmen and freedwomen had to decide whether to accept the surnames of their white owners or to adopt a fresh surname. In many cases, they wanted to shed the "first" (and only) name by which their white masters had called them. Some former slaves were so weary of being called always by first names, like children, that they avoided them altogether, substituting initials instead. A man who renamed himself Y. W. Johnson could pretty much count on being called "Y. W. Johnson" or "Mr. Johnson" rather than

"Jimmie." Even with the help of computers, then, it is a fool's errand to comb through all the census records of all the southwestern states for one particular mulatto man born about 1812 whose name we don't really know.

We are a fool.

"Sanford Shirkey" produces no matches with a person of the right age and race. Neither does "Sanford Reavis." One name at a time, then. First name "Sanford," black or mulatto, born between 1810 and 1814, gets us nothing. Neither does the surname "Reavis" with the same demographic constraints. The surname "Shirkey" gives exactly one result.

On June 23, 1880, Charles Butt, a 25-year old census-taker in Fayette County, Texas, was working his way through a rural neighborhood where white and black families lived on adjacent farms. At one house he interviewed a mulatto man, 69 years old, named Doctor Shirkey. Being a Butt, the census-taker had probably learned not to make wisecracks about peoples' names. If he was accustomed to calling all colored people by their first name, however, "Doctor" would have wrong-footed him. Mister Doctor Shirkey probably wasn't the richest mulatto in the Southwest. He was a farmer and a widower. He was feeling well that day, had no chronic illnesses, and was physically sound in every respect. He couldn't read or write. He had two daughters, Henrietta (age 10) and Emily (6). He also had two sons. The older one, Anderson (13), helped on the farm and sometimes went to school, though he hadn't yet learned to read. The younger one, eight years old, wasn't in school yet. His name was Sanford Shirkey.

Stewart Bridge, circa 1923

A Course in Applied Lynching

"And this also," said Marlow suddenly, "has been one of the dark places of the earth."

—Joseph Conrad

Two Crimes

In the opening years of the twentieth century, John Stewart, former Judge of the Boone County Court, stood at the edge of the University of Missouri campus and looked west at the rolling hills of his pastureland. He saw the future: a neighborhood of large modern houses, each architecturally unique, but suited to the others. Pre-wired houses, pre-plumbed and connected by miles of underground gas, water and sewer lines. Deep wooded lots, brick-paved streets, a little parkland for children and dogs to enjoy, all within walking distance of campus and downtown. Like many developers who followed him, he stood to make a fortune selling the good life to the residents of the city of Columbia.

There was an obstacle, however. Between the campus and Stewart's pasture was a ravine thirty feet deep, at the bottom of which lay Flat Branch Creek and the MKT rail-road tracks. When necessary, people scrambled down the side of the ravine, crossed the creek on mud-caked planks, and climbed up the other side, but this was not an appetizing prospect for the middle-class families he expected to attract. In 1906, in a gesture of shrewd generosity, he built a steel-and-concrete bridge across the ravine and donated it to the city. For a few years it was called Stewart's bridge, but gradually it became Stewart Bridge, and eventually it came to be identified not with the donor, but with an incident that three generations of Columbians have picked at like a scab.

THE YEAR was 1923. On Saturdays, cars and farm wagons lined the curbs and filled the parking lane in the center of Broadway. A few civil war veterans, mostly confederates, could still be mustered to lead the Memorial Day parade. To place a call on the new crankless phones, you lifted the ear-piece off its hook and waited for the central operator to ask, "Number, please?" The campus ROTC operated a commer-cial radio station, but at $250 retail, receivers were scarce. For news, Columbians relied on newspapers, three pub-lished in the city itself and others brought by train from Kansas City and St. Louis. To buy liquor, you went to a bootlegger. If you were black, you stepped off the sidewalk when whites approached, and if you were male, you removed your hat. Law-abiding whites seldom ventured into a black neighborhood, unless they were "friendly visitors" with Professor Ellwood's Public Welfare Society. In theory, blacks and women could hold public office and serve on juries, but in practice they didn't. A small set of prosperous white men dominated public life, and most others bore this dominance meekly.

Every Tuesday at noon, Walter Williams, founder of the Missouri School of Journalism, turned an hourglass at the center of the Round Table in the back room of Harris's Café, and nineteen of Columbia's most prominent men discussed local and world affairs until the hourglass emptied. A guest always filled the twentieth chair and led the discussion. If the guest was dull, the member who invited him was fined a dollar.

That Professor Hermann Almstedt was invited to the Round Table once shows he was viewed favorably by leading men of the community. That he was invited twice shows that whoever brought him didn't lose his dollar. The members must have appreciated his intelligence, culture and integrity. He didn't have wealth to recommend him, and if he had a sense of humor nobody seems to have noticed it. Learning, though, he had in abundance. During the Great War, when the University closed all German classes, Almstedt had taught French, Spanish, and Sanskrit instead. Now he had returned to German and was also directing the Men's Glee Club at the University. His idea of "glee" included Mendelssohn, Haydn, and Schumann, leavened by some European folk music. "No jazz, no trash, no silly stuff," a friend said admiringly.

Almstedt and his wife were raising a family of girls in a neighborhood west of Stewart Bridge. Like all the Almstedts, his 14-year-old daughter Regina was a musician. About 3:00 one Friday afternoon in April she was walking home from an after-school lesson. According to subsequent newspaper stories, she met a black man on the bridge. The man told her that a child was wandering down the MKT tracks and might be struck any minute by a train. Regina climbed down the slope and began to search the valley. When the man chased after her, she knew she had been trapped and started running through the woods and up a hill toward home. The man caught her by the ankle. She beat the umbrella she was carrying to pieces against his head and face. He punched her repeatedly and waved a knife, then took off his belt and looped it around her neck. Regina, hoping that robbery was his motive, threw all the money she had—half a dollar—on the ground, but the man said he wanted revenge on the white man who had stolen his wife: he intended to rape a white woman.

Then, the newspaper stories said, he changed his mind. He took the half-dollar, apologized, and ran down the tracks. Bruised and frightened, Regina fainted twice on her way home. When the police arrived, she described her assailant as a negro, 25-30 years old, with a mustache like Charlie Chaplin's and clothes that gave off a strong chemical smell.

Under the bridge, the police recovered a clue almost too good to be true: overalls that Regina said had been tucked under her attacker's arm. The Chief of Police, Ernest Rowland, borrowed a pair of bloodhounds and set them to work. One hound circled the valley haplessly, but the other picked up a scent immediately and followed it west through the woods, north through the brick-paved streets of white neighborhoods, then east through the dirt streets of Columbia's black business district. The hound led policemen straight through the door of George Scott's restaurant at the corner of 5th and Walnut. There it became confused. The policemen brought it out on the street again, and it seemed to pick up a trail heading east along Walnut. After following the scent for a few hundred feet, the hound stopped. Inquiries were fruitless. Apparently no one at the restaurant or in the neighborhood had noticed anything or anybody unusual. The police had reason to suspect that the assailant had ordered a meal.

THE CHARLIE Chaplin mustache was the next promising lead. Chief Rowland sent the Columbia police force into the black neighborhoods looking for a man who had one.

The afternoon after the assault they arrested a man in his mid-thirties, James T. Scott, a long-time Chicagoan who had moved to Columbia to be near his mother and stepfather. Since his arrival, he had filed for divorce, won custody of his two young children, and married a teacher at Douglass School. On the Fourth of August, 1922, though comparatively new in town, he had been one of the organizers and marshals of the Emancipation Day parade, leading two dozen bunting-draped trucks and automobiles, two bands, and hundreds of enthusiastic marchers through Columbia's downtown.

After the parade, there had been a picnic at the fairgrounds for thousands of citizens, several hundred of them blacks drawn from other towns in central Missouri. There were fireworks and music, and J. M. Calkins, the owner of an amusement park south of Columbia, sold rides on a merry-go-round he brought in for the occasion. When Calkins failed at the end of the day to pay the agreed $100 licensing fee, Scott and the other event organizers sued him. Calkins, who was white, demanded a jury trial, knowing that the jurors were certain to be white. But the white jury sided with Scott and his black associates, ending the story of Emancipation Day, 1922, with an unexpected exclamation point.

Scott—"Scotty" as some called him—had become a leading figure in the black community. Now he had also become a plausible suspect in the rape. He worked as a janitor at the University's School of Medicine, only a few hundred yards away from Stewart Bridge, and he wore a Charlie Chaplin mustache.

Chief Rowland brought him to the curb outside the Almstedt house. Regina stepped out onto the porch, at least thirty feet away: "Oh! Those are his eyes!" she cried. "Don't let him come any nearer!" The following afternoon, Rowland hid Regina in an anteroom of Prosecutor Ruby Hulen's office while Hulen interviewed four black prisoners. Regina, who couldn't see the men, shook her head during every interview but Scott's, and then indicated that she was sure he was the man. The four men were brought into the anteroom, and Regina picked Scott out of the lineup. Later, Rowland brought the girl vials of chemicals and asked if she could identify one as matching the smell of her assailant's clothing. When she sniffed the bottle containing formaldehyde, which was used to preserve specimens at the medical school, she recoiled and asked that the bottle be taken away immediately: "I can see him when I smell it!" Hulen and Rowland believed they had their man. Out-of-town sheriffs and police chiefs who were holding black men with suspicious mustaches were told that they could let their prisoners go.

Still, Prosecutor Hulen delayed giving the press the prisoner's name or the details of the investigation, and rumors took the place of concrete news. Many said that Regina had, contrary to the newspaper reports, been raped. In the house next door to Hulen's, 9-year-old Dorothy Nowell couldn't sleep at night. She was afraid that a black man would break through her window and do the terrible thing to her that he had done to her babysitter Regina— though her mother hadn't explained very clearly what the terrible thing was. She took an umbrella from a closet and propped it beside her bed so she would be ready to defend herself.

Men began to talk about a lynching, and some of this talk was reported in newspapers in Columbia and around the state. In such a heated atmosphere, Hulen realized, it was important not to point the finger at the wrong man, and Scott continued to insist that he was innocent. He claimed that he had been at work at the medical school all afternoon, and credible witnesses placed him there about 3:00 and again about 5:00. Strong as the case against Scott seemed, it depended entirely on the testimony of the young victim. What Hulen needed was a witness who could destroy Scott's alibi.

The city had immediately offered a $200 reward for information in the case; civic groups had soon raised $925 more, and Hulen applied to the state for $300 beyond that. At a time when farm labor typically paid three dollars a day, the total reward was enough to encourage cooperation. Chief Rowland sent his officers into the community looking for anyone who had seen Scott on the afternoon of April 20. The break came on Friday morning, April 27. A witness reported seeing Scott walking past the Dalton Coal Company at Fourth Street and Walnut about 4:15 on the afternoon of the assault. He was walking south (toward campus) with a bundle under his arm. The bundle was a curious detail, suggesting perhaps a man on an ordinary errand, but Hulen believed he had what he needed.

The Prosecutor moved quickly, informing both Scott and the Columbia *Daily Tribune* that a charge of assault would be filed that very afternoon. Just before 3:00, he brought Regina Almstedt to the courthouse so that she could again identify Scott in the presence of witnesses. Then he met with members of the Almstedt family to discuss Regina's testimony. No one present ever described the meeting publicly, but later events imply its content. Professor Almstedt made it clear that he was less interested in vengeance than in preventing more suffering. He had recognized soon after the attack that Regina could become an object of pity and unwelcome curiosity—a "ruined" girl, and perhaps an excuse for mob violence. He had kept his daughter quiet while she recovered, telling her story for her with the most disturbing details withheld. Unless and until a case went to court, there was no reason for Regina to speak about the unspeakable parts of her ordeal.

Prosecutor Hulen's timetable for the afternoon fell apart during this discussion. Apparently he was hearing for the first time that Regina had been raped; certainly he was learning a good deal about the quality of Hermann Almstedt's character. Reporters hoping for a late-breaking story waited for more than an hour. Deadlines passed, the court adjourned, and still the door to the Prosecutor's office stayed closed. It wasn't until 10:00 the next morning, Saturday, April 28, that Hulen appeared before Judge Collier. "Now comes the prosecuting attorney for the state," the record reads, "and files his information charging the defendant with the crime of rape."

THERE WAS time Friday evening and Saturday for influential men in the city to discuss the implications of Regina's changed story. It would be horrible for the girl to have to testify about what had been done to her—to say the words in a crowded courtroom, in front of slack-jawed farm hands and out-of-town reporters eager to print the sordid details. The rape had been tragedy enough, why must the Almstedt girl be humiliated again? How much happier everyone would be if the town could continue to believe, or even *pretend* to believe, that she had fended off the rapist with her umbrella.

Like most of the influential men, Ed Watson, owner and editor of the *Daily Tribune*, considered himself to be above bigotry. A month ago, he had run a front-page story exposing the Ku Klux Klan's unsuccessful attempt to organize a Columbia chapter and had ridiculed the Invisible Empire in a series of editorials. James Scott, though, was a rapist. Watson understood the feelings of men who wanted this crime to be dealt with immediately. "A man killer is a mild-mannered and desirable citizen compared with a despoiler and ravisher of innocent girlhood," he wrote, clamping his thick cigar in his mouth as he composed an editorial. He was sure it made no difference to him whether the rapist was black or white.

From the front page of the Columbia *Daily Tribune*, Saturday evening, April 28, 1923:

GIRL IDENTIFIES NEGRO ASSAILANT

* * *

Miss Almstedt Faces Scott and Declares He is the Guilty Man.

* * *

NEGRO GETS NERVOUS

* * *

Retains E. C. Anderson to Defend Him—Plea Will Be Not Guilty.

* * *

Miss Regina Almstedt, 14-year-old daughter of Dr. and Mrs. Herman B. Almstedt, yesterday positively identified James Scott as the negro who criminally assaulted her in a ravine south of Stewart's bridge on Friday afternoon, April 20.

Scott waived preliminary and appeared with his attorney, E. C. Anderson in circuit court this morning.

Judge H. A. Collier asked if his name was not James Scott and was informed that it was. The court ordered the name on the indictment changed from Charles to James.

Judge Collier set the case for trial on May 21. At that time Judge Ernest Gantt of Mexico will be on the bench and will try the case.

Mr. Anderson did not ask for a change of venue and has intimated that he will not do so but will try the case in Boone County.

Miss Almstedt, accompanied by her mother, went to the office of Prosecuting Attorney Hulen yesterday afternoon shortly after 3 o'clock. Scott was placed in the grand jury room in front of a window with the light shining full in his face. Sheriff Fred Brown sat to one side of him. Chief of Police Ernest Rowland stood behind the negro with one hand on his shoulder.

Miss Almstedt walked into the room with Mr. Hulen and her mother. She advanced to within three feet of the negro and looked him full in the face and turning to Mr. Hulen said; "I never want to see him again, he is the man."

Scott's face bears faint pox-marks and he has peculiar eyes. Miss Almstedt had never been close to the negro since the attack and when she was brought face-to-face with him she identified him without any hesitancy whatever.

Chief Rowland, who stood with his hand on the negro's shoulder, said that he trembled noticeably when faced by his accuser and that he became perceptibly nervous.

Scott has retained E. C. Anderson to defend him. Asked this morning what his plea would be, Mr. Anderson responded, "not guilty."

A witness has been found who saw Scott near Dalton's coal office on fourth street about 4:15 on the afternoon the crime was committed. Scott claims that he was at his work about the medical building during the entire afternoon of April 20. The witness says that Scott had a package under his arm. It is the belief of the officers that the negro had the clothes he wore when he attacked Miss Almstedt in the package and that he took them to the medical building and burned them.

It is generally believed that Scott is guilty of the crime and Miss Almstedt's identification makes certain now that he was the man who attacked her.

There has been much talk of mob activity and many men of sound judgment who do not believe in mob law are of the opinion that if it is positively proven that the negro is the man who committed the crime the taxpayers should be saved any costs that might accrue from a trial and that summary justice should be dealt to him.

BY COMPARISON to most blacks in Columbia, James and Gertrude Scott were well off. She taught a combined first and second grade class at Douglass School, earning about $75 per month, not much less than elementary teachers in white schools. He earned as much as the white janitors at the University: $65 a month. They rented a good house and owned a practically new Hupmobile, for which Scott had paid $600. So when it became clear that he needed a lawyer, he hired a good one: Emmett Anderson was the president of the county bar association. Scott signed over his Hupmobile as collateral.

Very likely it was Scott's minister, Reverend J. Lyle Caston, who recommended Anderson. It was definitely Caston who wanted George Vaughn, a black lawyer from St. Louis, added to the team. Vaughn was a battler. With his heavy shoulders, thick neck, and close-cropped hair, he wouldn't have looked out of place in a boxing ring. In 1948, newspapers across the nation would carry a picture of him at the Democratic National Convention, pumping his fist above his head as he demanded that the Mississippi delegation be unseated because it had endorsed the doctrine of white supremacy. Vaughn lost that fight, but a year later he won a landmark U. S. Supreme Court case that allowed blacks to buy property in neighborhoods with "white-only" covenants. Vaughn's brilliant brief in *Shelley v. Kraemer* became assigned reading at Harvard Law.

That, of course, was in the future, but Vaughn's accomplishments before 1923 were impressive enough. He was a power in St. Louis politics, a founder of the *Argus*, the city's principal black newspaper, and the chairman of the St. Louis NAACP. Photographs give a sense of how forceful, even intimidating, he might have been in person, arching his eyebrows and looking directly into the face of any man, black or white.

Caston can't have called Vaughn much before noon on the Saturday of the arraignment; he was on a train by 4:00. Caston met him at the Wabash station and they drove first to the parsonage for a quick meal, then to Stewart Bridge to study the scene of the alleged attack and to take measurements. The drive gave Vaughn an introduction to the racial topography of Columbia. Railroad Row, where they started, was an island of about 200 black residents in the northeast part of the city, separated from downtown by white neighborhoods around Christian College and the Columbia High School. Another 2000 blacks lived west of the city center in an area that Columbia's most polite whites called "colored town."

Colored town had its social and class divisions. The Sharp End, a downtown strip of black-owned pool halls, restaurants, and stores, had a reputation for toughness, though Reverend Caston's attractive Second Baptist Church was nearby. The West End, just north of downtown, was solidly middle class. James and Gertrude Scott lived there. The Cemetery Hill neighborhood, south of Broadway, was a disheartening slum. Here no one had a furnace, and the only running water came from outdoor taps shared by three or four households. Children played in sluggish Flat Branch Creek, an open sewer that carried effluent from feedlots, chicken runs, privies, and a meatpacking plant. Standing on Stewart Bridge in the diminishing twilight, Caston and Vaughn could look north over this shantytown. Beyond it, to the northeast, they could see the copper dome of the county courthouse. To the east, atop a hill, stood the gleaming white dome of the University's administration building and, above it, the rising moon, which was nearly full.

After examining the scene, Caston and Vaughn returned downtown to meet with Emmett Anderson in his offices on the third floor of the Guitar Building, close to the courthouse. Anderson had already found two white witnesses crucial to the defense. One had been working with Scott the afternoon of the attack. He would testify that the two of them had returned to the medical school at 3:10 after taking a truck loaded with dissecting-room cadavers to the incinerator. The other man would testify that he had seen Scott polishing floors and woodwork at 3:45. The alibi would hold, after all.

The three men talked late into the night about their strategy. About 11:00 there was a knock on the door. Anderson answered and stepped into the hallway. As the short conversation there broke up, Vaughn heard the visitor warn Anderson to be careful. When Anderson stepped back into the office, he explained that the man was a deputy sheriff who had apparently noticed the lights in the office and hurried over to deliver a warning. A mob was forming; there was talk about lynching Scott and other black prisoners in the jail. There was talk, even, about lynching Anderson. The three men scattered through the office, pulling chains to switch off the lights, then regrouped at a window overlooking the courthouse square. The moon, directly overhead now, was so bright that they could see the individual bricks that paved Walnut Street. On the near edge of the courthouse lawn, near the four Ionic columns that marked the site of the older courthouse, a dozen men and boys were talking. More men gathered around them, perhaps two dozen more, and the whole body hurried across the lawn toward the jail.

The years since the end of the Great War had been notable not only for lynchings but also for race riots, including a massacre in Tulsa two summers before. Reverend Caston immediately worried about his family. He and Vaughn left the office to check on their safety and found the streets and sidewalks full of people—men, boys, and a few women—heading toward the courthouse square. Shouts and cheers came from the vicinity of the jail. It didn't seem wise for two black men associated with Scott to make their way through the thick of the crowd, so Caston led Vaughn home via a detour, perhaps down the alley between Walnut and Broadway, which was lit only by the moon.

At 10:45, Sheriff Fred Brown was crossing the courthouse square near the jail when he met a crowd of about 400 men. The sheriff must have expected some sort of trouble: for the last six nights he hadn't returned to his home and his wife, but had slept as well as he could in the jailhouse. Though he wasn't old enough to have witnessed it, he knew the story of the last lynching in Columbia, thirty-four years earlier. Then a few masked men had entered the jail after midnight and taken a black teenager accused of rape. The mob had put a noose around the boy's neck and thrown him from a window in the courthouse. Passersby the next morning discovered the body hanging at the front door, just below the inscription carved in the lintel: "Oh Justice, when expelled from other habitations, make this thy dwelling place."

What the Sheriff might not have expected was so many unmasked faces. Some had been drinking—Brown could smell that—but most seemed sober enough. They demanded the key to Scott's cell. Brown refused to give it to them. Some of the men muttered that that Brown was a "nigger lover." Brown let that comment pass. "Wait for the trial," he said. "If you aren't satisfied with the verdict, I promise to let you have him then." Meanwhile, he didn't want any bloodshed. He told the men to disperse and saw a few walk away. Carrying his short nightstick but showing no firearm, he returned to the jail.

The mob withdrew. Several minutes later they attacked at what they might have thought a weak point, the jailer's quarters. If they could enter here, they would be very near Scott's cell. A brick crashed through the kitchen window and men started to batter the door. The jailer, Wilson Hall, shouted from inside the building: "This is my home. You can't go through here, and the first man who attempts it, I'll kill him." The men backed away, one saying, "Well, a man's got a right to defend his own home." Hall was relieved. As he said later, he didn't want to kill anyone and he didn't want to get killed himself.

The mob retreated for a few minutes, then swarmed the unguarded south door of the jail. With a heavy axe, some-one broke the padlock. The men at the front entered a dark corridor—apparently Brown or Hall had cut off power to the lights. Nearby was a steel cage with two white prisoners in it. The mob hammered on the bars of the cage and demanded to know where Scott was. The prisoners answered that the Sheriff had taken him to the Fulton jail for safekeeping.

The mob knew better. They pressed down the corridor toward the old stone part of the jailhouse, which Sheriff Brown had designated the "negro section." Two doors should have blocked their way: one a thick iron plate bolted on the opposite side, one a heavy steel grate locked into a steel frame. Either the iron door had been left unlocked or they had a key. The steel door, however, which looked like a castle's portcullis, was secure. They had brought sledge-hammers and chisels, and they set to work trying to sever the bolts that held the hinges.

A few Columbia policemen gathered to watch. Chief Rowland walked past the jail without stopping to look. When some of the spectators gathered in the courthouse square asked him why he didn't interfere, he told them that there was no way anyone could get at Scott.

The men in the mob were persistent, though. "Pour it into her, Red," one shouted as another hammered. "That's the stuff, hit her heavy," said another. A man holding a chisel had his hand mashed by a sledgehammer, withdrew for a few minutes, and returned with the hand wrapped in a handkerchief. The sound of the hammers carried for several blocks, audible on the courthouse lawn, on the streets of the Sharp End, even on the playground of Douglass School, but the bolts held up. About midnight, someone outside the jail shouted to the men inside, "We'll get an acetylene gas tank and torch."

ONCE REVEREND Caston was sure his family was safe, he and Vaughn walked back up Walnut Street toward the mob. The courthouse stood on a hill well above the level of the Sharp End, and with the moonlight striking the whole of its

51

west face, it seemed enormous. Vaughn and Caston encountered frightened knots of blacks in the streets, talking together and trying to understand what was happening. From time to time a shout would go up from the courthouse lawn.

"Will they get him?" someone asked.

"This is too bad!"

"Oh, what a shame!"

"I never thought this would happen in Columbia."

When they reached the square, they discovered that the crowd had spilled off the lawn and into the surrounding streets. They couldn't get close enough to see what was happening at the jail. The sledgehammers continued to pound, and Vaughn could hear some of the mob's leaders shouting encouragement and commands. For the most part, the white crowd was in high spirits, joking and laughing. "It was plain that it was out for an exclusive American holiday" Vaughn wrote later, "and it was having the time of its life." The Columbia police were clearly not going to intervene.

Some in the crowd were country people, in town for Saturday marketing and gossip. Vaughn knew too much about recent race-baiting in rural Missouri to look there for help. Some of the loudest laughers, though, appeared to be university students, and Vaughn was stung by their attitude. Worse yet, there was evidence that prominent men from the city must be present and countenancing the mob action. Vaughn noticed several expensive cars parked around the square, and while he watched, another drove up. Two well-dressed men stepped out and vanished into the crowd. If no one in Columbia was going to stop this crime, Vaughn thought, at least someone should be held responsible for it.

He made a note of the license number. Then he and Caston returned to the parsonage to do what no one else had thought to do: call the Governor.

Vaughn and Caston had met with Governor Hyde two years before to discuss the lynching of a teenager named Roy Hammond in the small city of Bowling Green. The Governor had listened gravely to the delegation's denunciation of the sheriff and his deputies. Hyde had already studied the lynching in detail. An Assistant Attorney General he sent to Bowling Green had demanded the exhumation of Roy Hammond's body and had discovered that it was riddled with bullets. The boy, whose crime amounted to asking a white girl to take off her clothes, had been hung from a small tree and used for target practice before he died. Hyde understood that the witnesses, citizens and deputies alike, had perjured themselves. The whole incident had sickened him; he hoped never to hear of another lynching in Missouri. "You have a friend on the ground," he had assured Vaughn, Caston, and their colleagues. He had seemed to mean it.

IT WAS after midnight. While they waited for the acetylene torch, the hammerers continued to work, and one of the two hinges of the portcullis finally snapped. The torch was carried in and lit, its blue-white flame illuminating the faces of the mob's leaders and casting their enormous, shifting shadows on the walls and the ceiling. The second bolt was quickly cut, then the locking mechanism in the center of the door. The mob pulled the door down with a clang and a shout. Sheriff Brown phoned Ruby Hulen to ask him to come to the jail to help control the mob. "They're about to get me," Brown told him.

The blowtorch was switched off. Two or three men walked cautiously up the dark corridor. There was danger now because near the end of this corridor was a short hallway leading to the jailer's kitchen. It, too, had double doors: a solid one on the kitchen side, a steel-grate one beside the cells. If Brown and Hall had opened the kitchen door and were waiting in ambush at the grate, they could fire almost point-blank on anyone who approached Scott's cell.

Inside the jailer's quarters, the phone rang: it was the long-distance operator from Jefferson City, putting through a call from the Governor. The Governor told Brown that he was aware of the situation and that he had ordered out Battery B of the National Guard. They were mustering at the Armory just across the street from the jail and would soon come to the Sheriff's aid. Meanwhile, the Governor asked the Sheriff to do everything in his power to keep Scott safe until the militia arrived.

THE MEN at the front of the mob found that the door to the kitchen was shut. They turned on their flashlights and examined the two cells at the corridor's end, both of which contained black prisoners. In one cell a man fell to his knees, blubbering and begging not to be lynched. He appeared not to have a mustache, though, and his cellmate clearly did.

During the delay, several other members of the mob started down the stone corridor carrying the unlit torch. Behind these came hundreds of men, packing the corridor so solidly that none could have turned around. It was very dark. The ends of cigarettes glowed, and when a man struck a match, the flame created a halo around his face. In a few minutes the torch was sparked again, and light flooded the two cells. Now there was no doubt which man was Scott. Men were just beginning to cut the lock on his cell door when the door to the jailer's kitchen opened, and Judge Henry Collier stepped up to the steel grate. At first the men with the torch, intent on their work, seemed not to notice him, but Sheriff Brown called out, "George Barkwell, won't you listen to Judge Collier."

Barkwell, a big, broad-shouldered man, was standing near the cell door. He raised his left hand and the men paused to listen to the judge's plea: "Men, you don't know what you're doing. This is a bad case, a very bad case, but we should let the man have a trial by jury. I've set the trial date myself. It's less than three weeks away, and I've no doubt it will be a speedy trial."

"Get the damned nigger!" someone shouted from the back of the crowd.

"We're going to hang this damned nigger, anyhow!" shouted someone near the front.

"Let a jury of your own people decide this man's guilt or innocence," Judge Collier pleaded.

"To hell with juries! We know juries. We'll be our own jury."

Collier tried another tack. "I speak in the name of the father of the girl, who has been wronged more than any of you. He wants this man to have a trial." By then the crowd was so noisy that his words were inaudible. Ruby Hulen appeared at the grate and shouted to make himself heard. The men should wait at least long enough for Hermann Almstedt to come and talk to them, he said. Someone in the back of the crowd yelled, "Bring him down here. We'll lynch him, too!" For a moment, though, the men in front seemed to waver. To defy the judge and the prosecuting attorney and to commit a crime right under their noses may have been more than they had bargained on.

Shouts came from the crowded corridor behind them: "Go ahead, get him out!" "What's the matter in there? Are you afraid of him?" A young man in shirtsleeves shouted from the corridor, "Let me through! I'll run the damned torch!" He pushed his way to the front, grabbed the torch, and began to cut. Suddenly, the corridor went black. A man who had been at the front of the mob all evening had cut the hose to the tank, saying that if the fools kept burning acetylene in the cramped space, they were going blow the place up. He tried to carry the tank away. An old man with a revolver in one hand pushed him back. "That tank is going to stay right here until we get that lock burned off."

By flashlight, someone refitted the hose and restarted the torch. The man in shirtsleeves finished cutting the lock, and men from the front of the mob went into the cell with flashlights. They grabbed Scott and pushed him back down the corridor, kicking and punching him as they went. They brought him out onto the courthouse lawn and then stood him under the jailer's porch light to confirm his identity. Men crowded onto the porch to get a look, standing on the porch swing and railings until they collapsed, bringing the flowerboxes down with them.

In the jailer's kitchen there was a brief, tense conference. George Vaughn, sifting through reports and rumors a few days later, believed that at this moment, Sheriff Brown wanted to recapture Scott from the mob and that Hulen opposed him. It isn't hard to imagine either man's reasoning. Brown saw that there were six lawmen in the jail at that point—himself, his deputy, two policemen, the judge, and the prosecutor. If they armed themselves and showed that were ready to fire on the mob, they could get the upper hand. Battery B would soon arrive to help, and some of the city's other policemen would probably rally to their side. Ruby Hulen disagreed: the crowd around the mob had grown enormous; most were merely curious spectators; if it came to gunfire, innocent people might be hurt or killed. As Prosecutor, Hulen was the ranking officer on the scene. When the Sheriff and the Prosecutor stepped onto the porch to deal with the mob, they went unarmed.

By then more than a thousand citizens were crowded around the jail and courthouse. Brown stood in the light and called for volunteers to help him preserve law and order. A car was waiting to take Scott to another jail, he said, if only men would step forward to help get him to it. No one stepped forward. Hulen begged the mob to let the court do its work, saying that he would work hard for a conviction and was confident he would get one. No one replied. Scott asked for a chance to see his father one last time. Someone in the crowd shouted, "Take him to Stewart Bridge. Hang him!" Another, noticing activity around the Armory, shouted, "Get him away from here; the militia is coming!" A third, armed with a rifle, approached a small group of black men who were watching the mob. "Beat it!" he yelled at them, and then fired his rifle into the air. The crowd panicked briefly, scattered, and reassembled as the core of the mob started south at a trot, leading Scott or dragging him when he was knocked off his feet. The rope burned Scott's neck and cut the hands of a man who held it. Most of the crowd followed Scott south through Columbia's downtown and along the edge of campus, retracing the route Regina Almstedt took the afternoon she was attacked. Others led the parade in their cars, honking and shouting. Policeman Pleas King was among those trailing the crowd. He must have been surprised when a broad-shouldered black man, neatly dressed in a suit and tie, stopped him to ask who the leader of the mob was. King didn't recognize the man, but by his side, easily recognizable in his owl-like spectacles, was Reverend Caston. "A man named Rollins," King answered, and then hurried after the crowd.

Colonel Williams and Captain Campbell had hurried to the Armory—just across the street from the jail—as soon as the Governor called. They had immediately started phoning the men of Battery B. Not everyone answered, of course. The Battery had a reputation for discipline problems, and some of the members were in the crowd. By 12:40, six half-dressed men had assembled in the Armory. Colonel Williams placed a long-distance call to his commander, General Raupp, in Jefferson City. While he waited for the connections to be made, he watched the crowd from the Armory's door. They were beginning to run south, and one of them told Williams that the leaders had taken two black prisoners from the jail. Just then, the call to Raupp went through. Williams explained the situation and held the handset out the door so the General could get a sense of the chaos— honking horns, shouts, the buzz of many voices. Clearly there was no way that Williams could assemble enough men to deal safely with a mob this size. General Raupp instructed Williams to report the news to the Governor.

GOVERNOR ARTHUR Hyde was a tall man, so remarkably thin and habitually erect that in a crowd he stood out like an exclamation mark. His double-breasted suits seemed almost to button behind him, and his nose was so conspicuous that it was a source of constant humor. "I acknowledge receipt of your clipping which deals with the intimate relation between big noses and brains," he wrote in a letter to one of his supporters.

> *For the life of me I cannot see why you sent this clipping to me. It is proverbial in my circle of friends that my nose is not big, and I can prove by eighty percent of the people of Missouri that I have no brains.*

He was an anomaly in Missouri politics. In an era when the big-city Democratic machines were dominant, he was a small-town Republican washed into office on the great national Republican tide of 1920. Before then he had held no elective office higher than Mayor of Princeton, Missouri, population 1500. In Princeton he had taught adult Sunday school classes at the Methodist church. Eventually his class had swelled to over two hundred, standing room only, and had to be moved to the large meeting room in the Mercer County Courthouse. His witty, morally demanding homilies formed the backbone of his stump speeches.

Hyde was the same unaffected man in the Governor's Mansion that he had been in Princeton. Unable to understand why the taxpayers of Missouri should pay for his family's meals, he paid the grocery bills himself and surprised the kitchen staff with his frugality. On inauguration day, he found the traditional stovepipe hat so embarrassingly grandiose that he carried it under his arm all evening rather than put it on his head. Hyde and his family were invited to a private dinner that evening by outgoing Governor Fredrick Gardner and his wife. When they arrived, Mrs. Gardner was appalled to discover that the mansion's harried butler had failed to put napkins on the table. Hyde's 9-year-old daughter Caroline tried to put her at ease: "Oh, it's okay, Mrs. Gardner; we never use them at home." The napkin story became one of Hyde's favorites.

Hyde carried a vest-pocket memorandum book, and on one of its pages these words were written in his miniscule, precise handwriting:

Matt. 22.39 –

Being questioned as to which is the greatest commandment, says first "Thou shalt love thy God with all thy heart, and with all thy soul and with all thy mind." And then says 39. "And a second like unto it is this, Thou shalt love thy neighbor as thyself".

How comply with second? Does it mean love sentimentally? – Then impossible to comply. Does it mean only those neighbors who are close to us?

The only compliance we can make is to give all people equal rights and equal liberty and equal opportunity with us; take no advantage; seek no favors; use no underhand methods. Win – personally – if you fairly can. Do good and help the needy, the lowly, the poor. This interpretation makes all men neighbors, and all equal with us. Who sincerely and honestly carries out this interpretation loves all men, and all men's rights, as himself and his rights.

This makes second commandment the highest and most ideal idea of personal rights, – and is the pure abstract theory of government of, by, and for the people.

The Governor wouldn't let Colonel Williams give up. Even if the battery couldn't be assembled, he said, Williams himself should follow the mob and do what he could to prevent violence. And if a crime were committed, he should get busy and gather evidence to aid the prosecution, which would be a vigorous one, even if the Attorney General had to go to Columbia in person to lead it. The Governor rang off. By now the main body of the mob was out of sight. Colonel Williams, Captain Campbell, and two sergeants ran after it.

HUNDREDS OF spectators had driven directly to the bridge and were waiting on its moonlit deck or in the shadowy ravine beneath. The mob brought Scott, bleeding from his nose and ears, to the railing on the south side. They would have hung him immediately, but someone had cut off part of the long rope around his neck, and what was left was too short to do the job properly. Scott, the mob, and perhaps two thousand spectators waited while a longer rope was brought. It had been the warmest spring anyone could remember, and now, even after 1:00 a.m., the air was pleasant. In intervals of quiet, those up on the bridge could hear an undergraduate playing his banjo on the porch of a fraternity house. Under an arc light, Scott began to plead for his life. He said that he was innocent, that he had a 15-year-old daughter of his own and could never do such a thing. He had never touched a white woman in his life, he said. That afternoon his cellmate Ollie Watson had confided in him that it was *he* who attacked Regina Almstedt. At least two men on the bridge were inclined to believe him. He sounded like a straight talker, they said. There should at least be a proper investigation. Impatient men in the crowd shouted that they wanted to "have it over" right now: "Throw him down to us." someone called from under the bridge, "We'll take care of him."

A heavyset man with thinning white hair made his way through the crowd: Hermann Almstedt. He addressed himself to the men surrounding Scott, strangers who probably couldn't remember his daughter's name. "I have been wounded to the very heart by this affair," he told them, "wounded far more than any of you. Don't besmirch your hands with this deed. I plead with you to let the law take its course with this man. I ask it of you in the name of law and order and the American flag." Some in the crowd hissed. "Shut up," one man warned, "or we'll lynch you, too." Almstedt left without another word.

A powerfully built man about six feet tall pushed through the crowd carrying a twenty-foot rope. Working silently in the middle of the noisy crowd, he removed the short rope from Scott's neck and used it to tie his hands behind his back. He tied one end of the longer rope to the railing and made a noose at the other end. When he put the noose around Scott's neck, Scott fell to his knees and prayed. Those standing nearest could hear the words: "O Lord, have mercy on an innocent man." The big man lifted him as easily as he might have lifted a child and sat him on top the four-foot railing. There were shouts and cheers from the crowd. About fifteen feet away, a woman stood on the railing to have a better view, a friend holding onto her skirt so she wouldn't fall. "Over the railing with him!" the woman screamed.

Scott had maintained throughout the night a remarkable composure. While the mob hammered at the steel door, he lay still on his bunk, wrapped in a prison blanket. When they broke into his cell and asked which of the inmates was James Scott, he identified himself, but said he was innocent of the crime of which he was accused. When they began to drag him to the bridge, he said that they needn't pull him; he would walk with them. Now, balanced on the edge of the railing, he said he would jump rather than be pushed. The big man pushed him hard. As he began to fall, he managed to say one last time, "I am innocent."

When Colonel Williams and his men rushed down Stewart Road, they could see that the bridge was packed solid and part of the crowd was spread south along the moonlit slopes of the ravine. Believing that the mob had decided to lynch Scott in the woods where Regina Almstedt had been attacked, Williams climbed down the slope into the shadows. Among the men at the foot of the bridge, he found a uniformed policeman. He asked the policeman where Scott and his abductors were. The policeman pointed straight up. Williams asked him if there was any way that Scott could be rescued. The policeman said no. Just then someone yelled, "Here he comes!" Williams looked up to see Scott's body hurtling down at him. The rope caught with a sickening pop; then twigs began to snap as Scott's feet struck the upper branches of a small tree. The corpse swung directly overhead, and for a moment the crowd was silent. Then Scott's legs kicked two or three times, convulsively, and Colonel Williams heard ripples of laughter around him.

A Hopeless Task

It was conceivable that the whole town was to blame. At the Broadway Methodist Church, the Reverend Joseph Randolph, descendant of John Randolph of Roanoke, descendant of Pocahontas, looked out on a congregation that could afford to be stylish—the young men in white trousers and bright bow ties, the women in spring suits or kimono-style dresses. Randolph knew where several of his parishioners had been the night before. The mob had swept past his house after midnight, enticing his son Jack to slip out a window and run down to the bridge, where he saw the crowd drinking and laughing and the police directing traffic. Reverend Randolph ordinarily preached a mild, pragmatic Christianity. This morning he was grim: "The seeds that we sow grow into fruit which we must reap. You cannot gather the seeds that you have scattered. It is a hopeless, utterly hopeless task. We have had a sowing in this community. God grant we may not have a reaping."

Professor Charles Ellwood, a pioneer in the new science of sociology, had been in downtown Columbia on Saturday morning, hearing heated conversations about James Scott's attack on Regina Almstedt, which more and more people were calling a rape. By noon, he was certain he was witnessing the formation of a mob. He called Mayor McDonald and urged him to take action immediately, before the situation got out of hand. The Mayor, like many of Columbia's other citizens, had long ago decided that

Ellwood—who meddled in the affairs of colored town and complained frequently about lax enforcement of liquor laws—was a crank. He assured the professor that there was nothing in the world to worry about.

But Professor Ellwood did worry. He worried, among other things, that people overestimated their ability to think for themselves and underestimated the power of the community to do their thinking for them. In his textbooks and classes, he compared individual minds to biological cells and the "group mind" to a complete organism. Under a microscope it might appear that the cells live autonomously, but take the microscope away and anyone can see that they are entirely dependent on the organism in which they live. Human minds are similarly dependent on the "group mind" of the community. That is why individuals seldom rise far above the moral plane of their tribe or neighborhood. "Civilized men act like savages in crowds," he explained to his students, especially when some event "excites the whole mass." Then all those individual minds unite into a single "creature of impulse, liable to follow any extreme suggestion."

In his criminology lecture two days after the lynching, Ellwood looked up at the undergraduates stacked in the rising rows of the amphitheater. This horrible incident, he told them, wasn't the result of one or two bad men deciding to commit a crime. It was a collective act that couldn't happen unless *many* members of the community willed it to happen. A student followed Ellwood to his office to ask a question: "Do you mean to say that a community in which a lynching occurs has lower moral ideals than the rest of the country?" Ellwood framed his response carefully, but the short answer was "yes." The student as it turned out, was a reporter for the St. Louis *Star*, which splashed the Professor's condemnation of Columbia at the top of its front page.

At the Columbia *Daily Tribune*, Ed Watson clamped his cigar in his mouth and pounded out an editorial response. Ellwood, he wrote, was "by no means a Sir Galahad." He was a "stock gambler." He had "dropped several thousand trying to guess the heads or tails of the market." He might "lay the Pharisaical unction to his soul that he is not like other Columbians," but he should remove the beam in his own eye before scratching at the mote in his neighbor's.

IN THE black neighborhoods, grief and blame took many forms. James Scott's mother, Sarah, had collapsed when she heard the news of her son's death. Friends had carried her to her bed and held her thrashing body down. "Oh, Lord, let me die! Oh, Lord, let me die!" she had wailed. Scott's brother Akers, Sarah's first-born, came from St. Louis to comfort her. Anna, Scott's teenage daughter from a former marriage, traveled from Chicago to join her younger siblings. She must have been shaken when she heard about her father's plea on the bridge: "I am innocent. I had nothing to do with this crime. How could I do such a thing when I am the father of a girl that age?" While the family gathered and grieved at Parker's funeral home, hundreds of men and women filed in to view Scott's body.

An eavesdropper on the whispered conversations of the black mourners would have heard a name not often mentioned in the white neighborhoods that week: Ollie Watson. Watson was a young cab driver in the Sharp End. A week before the attack on Regina Almstedt, he and a friend had offered a couple of girls walking downtown at lunchtime a ride back to Douglass School. Once they had the girls in the car, they took them out into the countryside and raped them. Watson's attack on Ernestine Huggard had been especially brutal: "sickening," people said, "unspeakable." The newspapers hadn't leapt to cover *this* rape, hadn't whipped the town into a frenzy. This was just a black girl, after all. The city hadn't offered a reward. The police had investigated at their leisure and eventually—ten days later—had arrested Watson, who became Scotty's cellmate. Scotty had said on the bridge that it was *Ollie Watson* who had attacked that white girl, and some in the black community believed it. If white Columbia had been half as concerned about Ernestine as it was about Regina, they said, Watson would have been arrested before the white girl was attacked and Scotty would still be alive.

A white mob had reached into the jail that night and snatched out an innocent man, leaving a real monster whimpering in his cell. Did anyone believe that a white prosecutor, a white judge, and a white jury would set these matters right? White Columbia was to blame for Scotty's death, and Ollie Watson was *doubly* to blame. Some of the men muttered that it might be time for a black mob to do the job right.

THOUGH RUBY Hulen had cousins scattered throughout Boone County, he was a newcomer to Columbia and not an easy man to understand. He wasn't gregarious. In an era when men built up social capital by participating in secret societies—Elks, Odd Fellows, Knights of Pythias—he didn't. When he ran for Prosecutor in 1920, he introduced himself by reprinting in the Columbia papers a curious short biography that had first appeared in the Centralia (Mo.) *Courier*:

> Ruby Hulen is making an earnest, determined and energetic campaign for the office of prosecuting attorney. Such has been his life from boyhood. He has fought his own battles since the age of 12. Starting out he worked on farms and sold papers on the streets of St. Louis. Since he was 15 he has had family responsibilities and has sent a sister through college. When he decided to become a lawyer, the university privilege was denied him because of lack of early education. Undiscouraged, he went to Kansas City and, working through the day, studied at night and graduated from the Kansas City School of Law with honors and was admitted to the bar in 1915. As a lawyer, he has done well: a plodder, resourceful, never giving up and always ready to debate. As a soldier, he served throughout the war with the 89th Division: overseas 14 months; he saw active service in the battles of St. Mihiel and Argonne Forest and the German Occupation. Born on a farm near Hallsville, practiced law for some time in Centralia before the war, and now located in Columbia, he is truly a native son and a loyal democrat. He was married June 4th, 1919, to Anna English of New York, having met her in France where she was doing work with the Red Cross. To those who have met 'Rube Hulen' for the first time during this campaign, we say 'by his record you may know him.'

Earnest . . . fought his own battles . . . privilege denied him . . . undiscouraged . . . a plodder: hardly a picture of exuberant optimism. The photograph above the advertisement, somewhat incongruously, shows Hulen in formal clothing, as if he were just returning from an evening at the opera. His prematurely receding hair makes his forehead seem large: not a bad-looking face, but too bland to be memorable.

After the election he and his wife had started a new life in a new house in the Westwood subdivision, a handsome place with an inviting front porch, rather large for a childless couple. The mortgage must have been a stretch for a man with no savings and a job that depended on the next election. Clearly, Hulen was anticipating a future more cheerful than his past, one that would fit comfortably into a neighborhood of professors, lawyers, merchants, and doctors.

Likely he imagined a career in elective office. When that dream evaporated, he entered politics via the back room. In the thirties, he served the Democratic Party by funneling favorable news stories and editorials to out-state papers. He became the chairman of the state party, organized campaign events, and secured tickets for VIP's. He sent poll watchers instructions on how to identify and disqualify Republican voters with criminal records, and told officeholders and patronage employees what percentage of their salary they were expected to contribute to the party. He managed a successful U. S. Senatorial campaign. In the early forties, when it appeared that federal courts might force the integration of the law school in Columbia, he helped in a small way to ensure that a "separate but equal" school was created at Lincoln University. His correspondence shows him to be useful, circumspect and self-effacing.

As he aged, he was increasingly troubled by insomnia and depression. Sometimes he returned from work after a stressful day, took a pistol from his dresser drawer, and unwound by killing rabbits and squirrels in his back yard. Eventually his party service was rewarded with an appointment to the federal bench in St. Louis, and for fourteen years he was an exemplary district judge: acute, frank, and even-handed. In 1957, in the midst of a vexing trial involving political corruption and influence peddling, Judge Hulen stepped out into his back yard and put a bullet through his head.

We know that Hulen went to Stewart Bridge the night of the lynching, though we don't know precisely when. Probably he stayed at the jail long enough to discuss Sheriff Brown's plans for protecting the prisoners the mob had left behind. He may have called Professor Almstedt to ask for his help. These delays would have put him on the scene too late to push his way onto the bridge and reach James Scott, but in time to hear the crowd's shouting, its brief silence, and the wave of laughter. Walking onto the deck of the fast-emptying bridge, he joined Colonel Williams, who was interviewing potential witnesses, but the remaining bystanders said that the lynch mob was gone and that they had recognized no one in it. The two men drove to the police station to call Governor Hyde.

The Governor and the Prosecutor were strangers. One was a Republican, one a Democrat. One was an outspoken critic of local law enforcement officers, one a novice county prosecutor. Their conversation that night was short and tense. Hulen explained that the mob had been relentless, that he had tried for half an hour to turn it away from violence, but that nothing could stop it. He told the Governor that he had seen the savage side of human nature in the War, but nothing like the fury he had just witnessed. Hyde offered Hulen all the help the state could give, from the assistance of the Attorney General to a declaration of martial law. Hulen assured the Governor that he could already name the leaders of the mob, and that he would have the case before a grand jury by Tuesday. He thanked the Governor for his offer of help, but said that he believed he had the situation under control.

Nonetheless, the Governor sent General Raupp and two other trustworthy investigators to Columbia before dawn and had the Attorney General assign his top assistant to the case before breakfast.

FROM THEIR beginning, grand juries have been less about achieving justice than about obtaining consent. In medieval England, leading men in a community assembled to decide which neighbors they were willing to turn over to the King's traveling magistrate. No judge presided over the grand jury, and no one represented the accused. Often, the jurors acted on rumor and reputation, not bothering to summon witnesses. If they issued an indictment, the magistrate applied whatever methods of trial were in fashion: the defendant might be thrown into a lake, for instance, to see whether he floated or sank.

As jurisprudence became more refined, trial by a "petit" jury replaced trial by ordeal. For centuries, though, the preliminary "grand" jury hearing remained a way to test whether community leaders would countenance prosecution. Criticism of the system stiffened in early twentieth century America partly because Southern grand juries refused to indict whites for crimes against blacks. By 1923 Missouri and many other states allowed prosecutors to take felony cases directly to trial, without grand jury indictments. Ruby Hulen could have filed murder charges against the ringleaders of the mob on his own authority. By electing to convene a grand jury, he was putting Columbia to a test. Were the leading men of the town ready to see white neighbors put on trial for the murder of a black man whom everyone knew to be a rapist?

Assistant Attorney General Henry Davis was at Hulen's door within eight hours of Scott's death. Davis was ten years older than Hulen and a much more experienced prosecutor. During the Great War, he had been a Colonel in the 89th Infantry, the division in which Hulen had served as a Lieutenant. The two men had waited through bombardments on the same battlefields, and they had common acquaintances, living and dead. In a photo taken the week after the lynching, the two stand shoulder-to-shoulder. Davis is a muscular man with a beetling brow and ears that lie flat against his skull. Put a whistle around his neck and he could be a football coach smiling confidently before the big game. Hulen, a few inches shorter, looks fragile. He hasn't bothered to remove his glasses for this photograph. His slender neck tilts slightly toward Davis, and he is frowning.

After a sleepless Saturday night, Hulen started early Sunday morning with Davis at his elbow, and worked until late Sunday night, alone in his office. Early Monday morning, he traveled to Jefferson City to confer with Davis and Attorney General Jesse Barrett. At midmorning, the three men offered an impromptu news conference. The Attorney General expressed confidence in the outcome: "I know the people of Boone County and I know that they are not the kind to let this assault upon law and order go unpunished." Hulen knew the people of Boone County too well to be so certain. "If they give me a jury who has any respect for the law, there will be indictments returned for those responsible for the lynching twenty-four hours after the jury meets," he said. *If.*

From Jefferson City, Hulen returned to Columbia and departed immediately for St. Louis, where the judge of the circuit court was recovering from colon surgery. Hulen went to the judge's bedside to get his signature on the order for a special grand jury. By 2:15 he was back in Columbia, instructing Sheriff Brown to draw up a list of jurors. That evening he drafted "informations" against two men he wanted to keep in jail, available for witnesses to identify, during the grand jury proceedings. Since he wanted to leave the murder charge to the grand jury, he accused the men, George Barkwell and Hamp Rowland, of helping an accused felon escape from the county jail. Hulen may have been too tired to relish the irony of this charge. After forty hours of almost continuous activity, he went home Monday with the prospect of a proper night's sleep.

JAMES SCOTT was buried in the Columbia Cemetery at 10:30 on Wednesday. At about the same time Ruby Hulen was in his office reading the mail. One envelope was post-marked Jonesboro, Arkansas. Hulen opened it and found a note written in pencil on paper torn from a cheap tablet.

4—30—1923
Some where on the road.

I left cansas City this morning on my road to
Jonesboro. In the Commercial Appeal i saw the
lynching of a negro. Look heare Mr. Prosecuting
Attorney just as it happen I tell you something
you had better let this negro business goe or you
will git some of the same. take it on yourself if
it had been your daughter you can get meaning
enough out of this to now take warning of a
negro

From K.K.K.

This wasn't the first threat Hulen had received. Usually, they were indirect: a man would report rumors that if Hulen didn't show more consideration for the feelings of Boone County citizens in this matter, he might feel the rope himself. Hulen had by now honed his response. "Tell them that when they come to look for me, they won't need an acetylene torch to get me."

His confidence had risen in the last two days. As he interviewed witnesses, he decided that there were just a few bad actors in the crowd. Most of these were toughs from Harrisburg, a town notorious for the sign posted on its outskirts: "Nigger, don't let the sun set on your head here!" They had recruited a few roughnecks from Columbia, but this wasn't, as some implied, a crime in which the whole city was complicit. The grand jurors would convene at 1:00. If they were willing to do their duty, he believed he could get murder indictments against the ringleaders—perhaps first-degree murder, perhaps second. He wasn't eager to expand the circle of guilt outward, looking for men who had committed lesser crimes.

About the time that Hulen was reading the Klan letter, Henry Davis was preparing a statement for the press. Davis was going for a big win against the advocates of lynching and mob rule. He wanted the grand jury to draw the circle of blame much wider than Hulen did: "The laws of Missouri make no distinction between accessory to murder and murder," he wrote. "The men who encouraged the act by word or even by gesture are as guilty of murder under the law as the man who threw the negro from the bridge." When he reached the Boone County Courthouse at noon, he presented his statement to reporters, fleshing it out with very concrete examples:

> Anyone in that mob that shouted encouragement to the leaders, or cried *'Let's go to Stewart Bridge!' 'Throw him over!' 'Let's hang him!'* and things like that are as guilty as the leaders and can be charged with first-degree murder.

Reporters saw immediately what an extraordinary statement this was. More than a hundred Boone Countians might be indictable under Davis's definition. Davis predicted that the grand jury would set two records in the courthouse that very afternoon: one for the first indictment ever in a Missouri lynching case, one for the fastest indictment anywhere in a case of lynching.

By 12:45, jurors and witnesses were coming through the doors steadily, the foyer echoing with footsteps and voices. A bailiff directed witnesses, more than twenty of them, to a third-floor waiting room. They would be called down one-by-one as the jury sent for them. The grand jurors, twelve as required by Missouri law, gathered in the large courtroom. Sheriff Brown had chosen men of substance. White-haired Ben Nowell was one, the owner of the city's most successful grocery. Nowell was the grandfather of the frightened 9-year-old who slept with an umbrella by her bedside. He was a member of the Walter Williams' Round Table. So was his friend Marshall Gordon, another juror. Gordon's farms and dairies cupped the city's southeast edge like a hand holding a ball. C. B. Rollins was there, retired banker and friend of the painter Thomas Hart Benton. He hadn't yet been elected to the Round Table, but he would fill the next available seat. Other jurors were an officer with another bank, merchants from three towns, and five wealthy farmers. Nine votes of twelve were needed to indict; four could block any action.

When all were seated, the acting circuit judge read the jury its charge, a combination of magnificent boilerplate from the Missouri statutes and material tailored to the particular trial.

> It is your duty to lay aside hatred, ill-will or malice on the one hand, or fear, favor or affection on the other hand, that might influence you in this investigation. It is not your province to pass judgment or to forgive or countenance any offense. . . . Regardless of what you may think individually, regardless of what elements in society may think, regardless of what customs in the past have been, it is your duty to consider these cases and follow the strict letter of the law, as written on the books, and return indictments in all cases where substantial evidence justifies it.

The judge explained that the Prosecuting Attorney and the Assistant Attorney General would be in the grand jury room only to help jurors examine witnesses and to clarify legal points. They were not to be present during discussions of whether to issue indictments. That was it; the gentlemen were on their own. The jurors left the courthouse briefly to view the scenes of the action, the county jail and the bridge. They returned, entered the grand jury room, and shut the door.

Reporters had nothing to do but wait on the benches in the foyer or stand on the steps outside, smoking and watching the clouds move in. A few citizens came to the courthouse on routine business or to use the restrooms, but there was no curious crowd. The reporters drafted paragraphs about Davis's statement, about the threat to Hulen, about comments witnesses had made before giving testimony. They waited until their deadlines expired. There were no indictments that day.

When the indictments finally came down the next day, they were plainly the result of compromises. George Barkwell alone was charged with first-degree murder. Four other men, including Hamp Rowland, the brother of the police chief, were charged with obstructing an officer.

The immediate effect on the county was to rally supporters of the men accused. When Hamp Rowland turned himself in at the courthouse Friday afternoon, he was escorted by a ten-car caravan of friends from Hallsville. So many men poured into the sheriff's office to sign the bond that the clerk pasted on an extra sheet to make room for their names. Rowland, six inches taller than most of those around him, with a striking scar across his right cheek, obviously enjoyed the attention. "You're dressed up today, Hamp," someone said. "Yes," answered Rowland, smiling.

"I borrowed a suit of clothes to come in." One of his bondsmen was Marion Rollins, evidently the "man named Rollins" identified by Pleas King as the leader of the mob. The next year, when Rollins carried a pistol into a black dance party and killed a man, Rowland signed Rollins' bond.

George Barkwell's bailment the following Monday was less festive, but his bondsmen were wealthier and more distinguished. Chief among them was S. F. Conley, a lean man with thin gray hair and a smudge of mustache on his upper lip. A member of the Round Table and the owner of a palazzo in the Italian Renaissance style, Conley wore a sling on his right arm. It had been injured in a fall, he explained to a curious reporter, heading off speculation about a sledgehammer injury. Sheriff Brown held the paper steady while Conley signed awkwardly with his left hand. William A. Bright, President of Boone County Trust Company, was also a bondsman. "Fred," Bright told the Sheriff, "if any more of the fellows who were in that mob come up here for bond, you send for me. I'll make bond for them until you fellows around the courthouse holler 'enough!'"

"I WISH the papers would let the matter rest now," Sheriff Brown had said the day after the lynching. "The Columbia *Tribune*, I think, said enough before this thing came off." After Barkwell's bailment, the local papers were remarkably docile. None revealed that Hulen had charged James Scott with rape; none criticized the grand jury for announcing that its work was unfinished and then recessing indefinitely. Papers in New York, Washington, Denver, and Atlanta that had reported the lynching soon lost interest.

Only the black press remained focused on the story. W. E. B. Du Bois wrote a biting editorial for *The Crisis*:

> We are glad to note that the University of Missouri has opened a course in Applied Lynching. Many of our American Universities have long defended the institution, but they have not been frank or brave enough actually to arrange a mob murder so that students could see it in detail.

The Chicago *Defender* ran a cartoon under the title "College Sports." The top panel showed a black runner breaking the tape ahead of a white opponent at the Penn State relays; the bottom panel showed a crowd of white Missouri undergrads cheering the sight of a black man hanging from a ramshackle bridge.

HENRY DAVIS was a born crusader. One of the happiest days of his life had been spent northwest of Verdun, watching the advance of the American First Army from the passenger seat of a mail plane. "The shell holes," he recalled later, "made the earth look like one vast pepper box. The long lines of trenches, the destroyed villages, the road with long columns of troops and convoys of trucks were very visible." After days huddling in trenches, this vision of the grand battle spread out in the sunlight exhilarated him. Later, as an officer in the Judge Advocate General Corps, he had helped manage the occupation of Belgium and Germany. This, too, had been exhilarating. He was proud to be part of an army that lived up to its principles. "Now that there is no more fighting," he wrote to a friend at home, "the soldier, though in the country of his enemy, treats the inhabitants according to the principles of the Golden Rule. The people here dreaded our invasion of their territory, but upon our arrival, they became so enamored of the American ideal of the 'square deal' that they have been known to meet in council and declare that they want a Government like ours."

In the mountain village of Arlon he had seen a 1500-year-old tower that had been built by the slave-workers of an occupying army from Rome, and he had touched a wall pocked with bullet holes where an occupying German army had executed 162 Belgians "for no other reason than that they were loyal to their country." He understood that when George Barkwell went to trial soon after the Fourth of July holiday, America's claim to stand for something higher than the ancient rule of force would also be tried. Defense lawyers would imply that it was necessary, even right, for white men to take the law into their own hands sometimes, especially when a black man had turned violent and a white girl had been raped. The prosecution would have to join battle on this ground, arguing that *every* American deserved due process. A Boone County jury might be reluctant to apply the Golden Rule to James Scott, but to a crusader like Davis this difficulty made the case ideal. To show that the mob law was unjustified in this case would be to show that it was never justified.

The way to begin was to re-examine with a skeptical eye the case against Scott. Chief Ernest Rowland had led the investigation. He was the brother of one of the mob's leaders and had refused to defend the jail on the night of the lynching. One might reasonably wonder if he had conducted an unbiased investigation. At the heart of the case he developed against Scott were the triple identifications by Regina Almstedt. The identification by scent, which had seemed so impressive as presented in the *Tribune,* had in fact been shoddy. Rowland had brought only two vials of chemicals to the Almstedt house. The first contained pleasant-smelling oil of cedar, the second formaldehyde. The girl, primed to react to a noxious smell, would obviously choose the formaldehyde. If the second smell had been gasoline or ammonia, she would likely have chosen it instead. The identification by sight was similarly flawed. Rowland had brought Scott to the Almstedt house within twenty-four hours of a traumatic attack and asked the girl if this was the man who attacked her. Not having looked steadily into the faces of many black men in her entire life, she had looked at this black face in a moment of tremendous stress and said "yes." "Yes" was a step toward putting the incident behind her. "No" would have meant looking into the faces of more black men. As for the identification of Scott by voice, it was worth remembering that she was identifying a man she had seen just the day before and might have heard speaking. It was also worth remembering that she was sitting in a room with Chief Rowland, whose desire to build a case against Scott may have led him to raise an eyebrow when his principal suspect spoke, or to look at Regina with obvious anticipation.

But pointing out weaknesses in the identification would strike many Columbians as mere hair-splitting. A black man had attacked Regina Almstedt, and white citizens would cling to the idea that Scott was guilty unless Davis and Hulen offered another black suspect in his place. On the bridge, Scott had named Ollie Watson as the culprit. Was it possible that he was telling the truth? The case against Watson for the rape of Ernestine Huggard seemed solid. It was plausible, at least, that a man who had entrapped and raped a 15-year-old black girl one Friday afternoon would entrap and rape a 14-year-old white girl the next.

Davis, by disposition and circumstance, was inclined to push the accelerator. Hulen had reasons to keep a foot on the brake. If Chief Rowland had chased after the wrong suspect in the initial investigation, Hulen had followed close behind. It was Hulen, after all, who filed the charge. The psychological cost to Hulen of changing his mind at this point was enormous. He would have to admit, first to himself and then to the world, that he had wrongly accused James Scott and so was partly to blame for the man's death. And there was something perhaps more awful to consider. There wouldn't be sufficient evidence to charge Ollie Watson unless Regina Almstedt identified him. Hulen would have to discuss with her the possibility that she had wrongly identified an innocent man who died as a result. She would have to go to the Audrain County jail in the nearby town of Mexico to try to identify Watson. And then, if it came to a trial, she would have to endure the cross-examination of Watson's defense attorney, George Starrett, who would remind the jury that this was the girl who had positively identified another man—a dead man now—as her attacker.

Hulen nibbled at the edges of the investigation, delaying the moment when he would have to discuss it with Regina and her family. There was the mustache to consider. That was one detail Regina was sure of from the start, and Watson was obviously clean-shaven. But that objection ended up strengthening the case: men who knew Watson reported that he had worn a mustache earlier in the spring, but had shaved it off just before he was arrested. In late June, Hulen contacted the Sheriff in Mexico and explained the situation. He would bring Regina Almstedt quietly to the jail in early July, and in the meanwhile, he had a favor to ask. He wanted Ollie Watson to grow a mustache, so the jailer mustn't allow him to shave or be shaved, except as Hulen specified.

Perhaps Watson guessed the meaning of his jailer's odd behavior. Mysteriously, his mustache refused to grow. The jailer developed theories. Prisoners had opportunities to smoke: perhaps Watson was using a match to singe the whiskers off every day. Or perhaps he plucked them with his fingernails or even abraded them away with a stone. For whatever reason, the upper lip stayed hairless. On 5th of July, four days before the Barkwell trial was to begin, Hulen took Regina and her parents to Mexico. The girl was able to observe Watson without being observed herself. When she emerged from the jail, reporters were waiting, but the wall of secrecy was impenetrable. The Almstedts passed the reporters without speaking. Hulen paused, poker-faced: "I have nothing to say at this time. I will make a statement perhaps a little later on."

The St. Louis papers soon reported that Regina had positively identified Watson as her attacker and that two other witnesses had seen him on the bridge that afternoon. Suddenly the town was abuzz with talk that James Scott was no criminal, but the innocent victim of a misguided mob. Barkwell's defense team was outflanked and outraged. Hulen might be bluffing, but there was no legal maneuver that could make him show his hand.

The *Tribune*, sympathetic with the defense, did what it could. It ran a front-page story in which Chief Rowland defended his investigation, saying that Regina Almstedt's identification of Scott had been so definite that it was "senseless" to dispute it. The next day it ran another front-page story headlined "OLLIE WATSON SAYS HE HAS COMPLETE ALIBI." He had been in or around George Scott's restaurant all afternoon, Watson had told a *Tribune* reporter, doing engine work on his cab with the help of his friend "Pig" Emery. George Scott confirmed this alibi: Watson, he said, had been in the restaurant often that afternoon. Pig Emery was unavailable for comment. Nobody mentioned the bloodhound, though he had been in the restaurant, too.

The Trial

After the record heat of April and the record cold of May, the weather righted itself. Wheat was harvested by the first of July, and corn was beginning to tassel. The Elks had planned a big Fourth of July fundraiser at Gordon Mansion just east of town, but light rain moved in, and by mid-day they decided they would have to cancel. If the rain came to a tenth of an inch by 9:00 p.m., they would collect $600 in cancellation insurance; otherwise they were out-of-pocket. While drops accumulated in the rain gauges, knots of citizens gathered on the sidewalks outside the offices of the *Tribune* and the *Missourian*. Neither paper was publishing that day, but both had reporters standing in their doorways describing the big Dempsey-Gibbons prizefight in Montana blow-by-blow as it came over the telegraph wires. To Ed Watson's delight, the *Tribune*'s wire service flattened the *Missourian*'s, reporting that Dempsey had won the fifteen-round decision while the *Missourian* still had him in the twelfth round, clinching Gibbons and punishing him with rabbit punches to the back of the neck. The rain stopped just short of the insurer's limit. The Elks rescheduled their picnic for the next day, and merchants closed their stores early to encourage attendance. More than 6,000 people turned out. Miss Belmont thrilled the crowd by jumping from her balloon and performing parachute stunts on her way down. Politicians hobnobbed and shook hands. The midway and the barbecue pits were busy, and the animal show played twice to packed houses. Contributors to George Barkwell's defense fund urged friends to chip in. When the fireworks exploded over the lake, oohs and aahs could be heard all the way to the courthouse, and the dancing continued until midnight.

George Starrett, Exalted Ruler of the Columbia Elks Lodge and member of George Barkwell's defense team, was in his element. He loved speeches and patriotic displays. As extroverted as Ruby Hulen was introverted, he had held one public office after another since 1916 and would continue to do so until 1941. Throughout his career he was a favorite speaker at men's church groups, where he assured his audience that he had never seen the son of a church-going father in a penitentiary, and at meetings of the Daughters of the American Revolution, where he shared with the ladies his conviction that the Flag and the D.A.R. were the two grandest institutions in the country. An accomplished ham actor, he performed dramatic readings at meetings of social and artistic clubs. His capacity for fun seemed inexhaustible: eleven years after the Barkwell trial, as a 50-year-old probate judge, he played in a charity baseball game, hit the winning home run, and bounced around the bases on a donkey name John Dillinger. "We were robbed!" his opponents hooted. Not everyone liked George Starrett, but everyone agreed that he had a reputation for being likable. That melancholy Ruby Hulen had unseated him as Prosecutor seemed almost an interruption of natural law.

Independence Day was a bittersweet holiday among black Columbians, a few of whom were former slaves and many of whom felt less than free sixty years after Emancipation. The lynching of James Scott was a reminder of their true condition. The upcoming trial of George Barkwell was very likely to be another. "Rev. J. L. Caston preached a very interesting sermon Sunday morning," a Columbia correspondent wrote to the St. Louis *Argus*. "He gave wholesome instruction for the Race, which we needed."

THERE HAD been talk of postponing the Barkwell trial until fall because the large courtroom on the west side of the courthouse was always an oven in mid-summer. Delay was unacceptable, though, and the trial was scheduled for the morning of July 9. By 8:30 spectators filled the benches in the back of the room, watching the lawyers and reporters on the other side of the railing. Henry Davis was there, eagerly talking with the press. "We expect to show by evidence that Barkwell was the man who placed the rope around the negro's neck and pushed him from the railing of Stewart Bridge," he told reporters. In all probability, he told them, Ollie Watson would soon be charged as the true perpetrator of the crime for which the mob had lynched James Scott: "I understand that Prosecuting Attorney Hulen does not desire to take action until the cases against Barkwell and the other four defendants are disposed of." Judge Ernest Gantt watched this impromptu news conference from the imposing oak desk usually occupied by Circuit Judge David Harris. Gantt had come from Audrain County as a substitute because Barkwell's lawyers claimed Harris was biased against their client. At 9:08 Judge Gantt brought the court to order, and more spectators crowded in, filling all the benches and then ranging themselves first along the back wall and then along the sides. Eventually there were 400 of them.

What they came to watch that Monday morning wasn't the trial itself, but the *voir dire*—the "truth saying" by which the court attempts to weed from the jury pool (the *venire*) those unsuited to sit in judgment. Judge Gantt's task was to empanel 40 men. Once this was done, the prosecution would cull 8 and the defense 20 more, leaving the 12 jurymen. In a typical trial the *voir dire* could be completed well before lunch.

Judge Gantt summoned the first twelve veniremen to the jury box, and the questioning began. Henry Davis directed his first question to Joe Baumgartner, a farmer: "Were you in Columbia on April 28th, or the early morning of the 29th?" Baumgartner was not. Nor had he heard the case discussed or talked to any witnesses. "Have you formed an opinion as to the guilt or innocence of this defendant, such as could not be removed by evidence you might hear during the trial, if you were accepted on the jury which will try it?" Baumgartner thought the long question over. He didn't know whether he had or hadn't, he said, but he was convinced that the case shouldn't have been prosecuted in the first place. Some spectators voiced their approval. This was enough for Davis: he turned to Judge Gantt and said, "I think, your honor, this man is disqualified."

Gantt may have welcomed the opportunity to take control of the pace and procedure in this unfamiliar courtroom. He told Davis that the court would hear the answers of all twelve men in the group before deciding who would be disqualified. The next two men questioned were farmers who said that mobs were sometimes justified in taking the law into their own hands. Some spectators applauded. A fourth farmer won no applause when he firmly opposed mob law and said he could render an impartial verdict.

Now Davis came to Isadore Barth, the most distinguished figure among the veniremen, an elegantly dressed merchant with a gold watch chain threaded through a buttonhole of his vest. Barth, a member of the Round Table, had the nonchalance of someone accustomed to deference. Yes, he was well acquainted with the case, he assured Davis. He had read about it, heard it discussed, and expressed his own views. He knew Barkwell personally through his business. His definite, strong opinion was that the man was innocent, and he had contributed to a fund to underwrite his defense. He didn't believe the case should ever have come to trial. If he were to become a juror, however, he would be broad enough to render a verdict according to the law and the evidence. Davis couldn't have relished this testimonial for Barkwell; he moved quickly to the next man in the box.

Seven men in the first twelve said that they believed in mob law—a declaration always greeted by applause or cheers—or that Barkwell should not have been charged. Two said that they would be reluctant to convict a white man for a crime against a black. Gantt listened patiently. He never censured an opinion, and he allowed the spectators' defiant cheers to encourage potential jurors to express whatever contempt for law they had in them. He asked questions of his own, particularly of one young farmer. "I'm not in favor of mob law," the man told him, "but if I'd been the daddy of the child, there wouldn't have had to have been any mob law." This man would do. He seemed honest and

89

plainspoken, and if jurors had to be saints, there could never be a trial in Missouri. Gantt found four men of the first twelve to be qualified.

By noon, it was clear that the venire would be depleted before 40 men qualified, so Gantt sent officers into the community to summon bystanders for immediate jury duty. Ordinarily this would have been Sheriff Brown's job, but the defense team, convinced that Brown was biased against Barkwell, had had him barred from duties associated with the trial. Lawyers for the two sides had to find some law-man they would trust with the duty, and they settled on Wilson Hall, the jailer. Hall and Officer Pleas King, his chosen deputy, returned from the lunch hour with fifteen citizens in tow.

As the afternoon wore on, the temperature in the crowded courtroom reached a hundred degrees. Refined men like old Ben Nowell occasionally withdrew linen handkerchiefs from their suit jackets and dabbed at their foreheads. Farmers reached into their hip pockets for larger cotton handkerchiefs and swabbed their faces and the backs of their necks. Judge Gantt was middle-aged and somewhat overweight. He must have suffered under his black robe, but he remained composed and attentive as the potential jurors unfolded their theories of justice. Spectators slipped out of the room occasionally for a smoke and a breath of air, but there were always plenty present to cheer a potential juror who declared that men sometimes had a right to take the law into their own hands. At 4:15, the court reached the bottom of the jury pool. Seventy-five men had been questioned; thirty-four had qualified.

That evening Deputy Hall and Officer King drove out of town, summoning potential jurors in the southern and western parts of the county. Twenty-one were in the courthouse at 9:00 Tuesday. The first six were called to the jury box and the *voir dire* stumbled forward. One man was too deaf to serve. A second said that if Regina Almstedt had been his daughter, he would have been leading the mob. When Ruby Hulen asked a third man whether he was related to anyone involved in the case, he declared that he was, in fact, a relative of Hulen himself. A fourth said that it was philosophically impossible for him to conclude that Barkwell was guiltier than any other member of the mob that night. "Would you feel that you were trying all the defendants?" Judge Gantt asked. No, the man answered, he could *try* Barkwell separately, but he didn't see how he could *sentence* him separately. A barber named Everman observed that the slow movement of the justice system was justification enough for lynching and that the mob "did the right thing," a sentiment that drew the usual applause. When the judge asked if anyone in the jury box had contributed to Barkwell's defense fund, Everman said that he hadn't yet, but he would as soon as someone asked him. He was also a relative of Hulen's, he added. Davis smiled: "Apparently, the Prosecuting Attorney has a good many relatives around here." A third man in the jury box immediately claimed Hulen as a relation. Two men from this group qualified. Gantt needed four more.

The next group was the worst. While spectators applauded and cheered, everyone in it declared himself in favor of mob law under some circumstances. As Judge Gantt dismissed the entire group, someone in the crowd laughed aloud, and the laughter spread quickly through the packed courtroom. Judge Gantt, who had tolerated insolence and childishness for two days, pounded the desk with his fist. "Stop that laughing!" he shouted. "This is not a frolic! A man is being tried for his life and liberty!" He glared at the spectators, a red-faced man with sweat on his balding forehead and his fleshy neck. "Mr. Sheriff!" he shouted—though Sheriff Brown had been barred from the courtroom—"if there is another demonstration of that kind, bring them forward and the court will deal with them."

SPECTATORS PACKED into the courtroom Wednesday morning well before the trial began, while the court was pulling from the jury pool the men rejected by the defense. This morning there were at least 500 people wedged into the benches and lining the walls. Most were white men, though about fifty women were scattered through the crowd, and a few black men sat together on one side. About 10:30, the hum of conversation ended. Judge Gantt administered the oath to the twelve remaining jurors and sent them into the jury box. He warned onlookers that no disruptions would be allowed during the trial, and that anyone unable to maintain silence would be ejected. Mr. Hulen, he believed, would present the opening statement for the prosecution.

Hulen's statement contained no surprises. He told the jury that the testimony of the state's witnesses "would trace Barkwell from the columns of the courthouse to the bridge" and "show that Barkwell placed the rope around the neck of the negro and pushed him over backward from Stewart Bridge."

> The evidence will show that this defendant and others
> indicted were not only the leaders but that they were
> practically the only ones who did active work. I think
> the evidence will show that this defendant committed
> the actual act of hanging at the bridge. But even if the
> evidence as to this defendant should only show his
> conduct at the jail, the state will expect a verdict of
> guilty.

Hulen described the ringleaders' hours of systematic work in breaking into the jail and burning the lock off Scott's cell door. He emphasized their refusal to heed the pleas of law enforcement officers and of Hermann Almstedt, the father of the girl attacked. He noted Scott's composure in his cell and his insistence that he was an innocent man.

Senator Frank Harris rose for the defense. His starched collar looked doubly white against his deeply tanned neck. Having retired from the state senate a year ago and declined a chance to run for Congress, he had been working hard on his golf game. He began by telling the jury the story of George Barkwell's life, how he had become one of Columbia's leading businessmen by dint of hard work and square dealing, how he had been elected to the City Council. He was no stranger to Columbia, and he was known to be a decent, law-abiding man. Now, to the matter at hand. "I believe the evidence will show that the deceased in this case is a negro. Just a few days prior to the alleged lynching, he was charged with the heinous crime of rape. I think the evidence will show that a heinous offense had been committed on a 14-year-old white girl." Hulen objected: the supposed crime of the man killed by the mob was irrelevant to the case. Judge Gantt overruled.

Harris went on to tell the jury about Regina Almstedt's meeting a black man on Stewart Bridge, about his luring her into the ravine below, about his removing his belt and making it a noose around her neck. Now Harris presented details that hadn't been printed in the newspapers. The black assailant had cut away the girl's underpants with a knife and, Harris believed, "accomplished his purpose." Harris was a skillful speaker; he would have paused here.

"Two colored men," he continued, "were taken to her home the next day, and the girl said that neither of them was guilty. Then the third was brought, and the girl went into hysterics, and said that he was the man. The third man was this man Scott."

He described the two other times Regina had identified Scott. "The girl described him as having an odor, and after she had been allowed to smell several odors of medicines, she said instantly upon smelling iodoform that that was it. This was the odor that Scott got in the Medical Building where he worked. The officers have held these things up that I have outlined. The statement that identification was positive was given to the press, and the press came out with the positive statement that Scott was guilty." By Saturday night, Harris said, "feeling was running high. The crowd grew and grew, and there were at least 1500 people around the jail when Scott was brought out."

Harris had the jury's complete attention, and at this point, he delivered his rabbit punch. He told the jurors and the packed, hushed audience that Ruby Hulen, the Prosecutor himself, had stepped out of the jail that night to address the crowd. He had asked them a question: *"Is there one person here who does not think that this man should be hanged?!"*

"I didn't say that!" Hulen protested.

Senator Harris—he retained the title for years after he left office—didn't miss a beat. "Then I withdraw it," he said, and went smoothly on. Judge Collier, he said, had pleaded with the crowd that night, *as had George Barkwell*, the man now wrongly accused of the crime. "He did nothing more at the jail than any of the other spectators, and I think that the testimony will show that the defendant did not touch the deceased at Stewart Bridge. He was standing on the other side of the bridge when Scott was thrown over the rail, talking to some people. I think the evidence will show that he did not enter into any conspiracy or anything of the kind to take the life of this man."

Because the trial had started late in the morning, the court recessed for lunch soon after the opening statements, allowing Hulen time to regain his composure and confer with Davis. Now the defense strategy was clear. Their overt argument would be that their client didn't kill James Scott. Their covert arguments would be that (1) even if Barkwell did hang Scott, the man got exactly what was coming to him and (2) it was unfair to single Barkwell out for punishment when so many encouraged the lynching—the newspapers, the sheriff, the crowd of onlookers and, yes, *even the Prosecutor himself.*

AFTER LUNCH, spectators crowded back into the courtroom, which was more oppressively hot than the day before. The humidity neared 100%; everyone could feel a storm coming; they pushed at the heavy air with fans and newspapers.

The general opinion in the Attorney General's office was that local juries resented a man from the State directing the case against one of their neighbors. Therefore, though Davis was a far more experienced lawyer and a better public speaker, Hulen took the lead for the prosecution. He called local law enforcement officers first. Sheriff Brown, Judge Collier, Deputy Hall, and Officers King and Miller confirmed that they had seen Barkwell at the head of the mob, along with the four other men indicted. None saw Barkwell touch the prisoner, the acetylene torch, or the cell, but all said that he had stood beside those who did. Barkwell's raised left hand had delayed the assault on Scott's cell while Collier and Hulen spoke to the mob. After Barkwell enforced this delay, Officer King testified, someone in the crowd shouted, "Don't let them out-talk you, George!" and the mob recommenced its work. "It looked like Barkwell was kind of directing the boys," King said.

Barkwell's lawyers left the substance of this testimony uncontested. Their cross-examinations focused instead on the conduct of Sheriff Brown. Congressman Sam C. Major, the senior member of the defense team, asked Brown if he had had *no information at all* to warn him that there would be an attack on the jail that night. "None I thought worth considering," Brown answered. Congressman Major, a man in his mid-fifties who scowled fiercely when he sat for portraits, didn't let that answer pass. He hammered Brown with a series of questions pointing out the strangeness of this answer, given that everyone else in the county, certainly everyone who could read a newspaper, seemed to expect a lynching. Ruby Hulen objected to each question. Judge Gantt allowed them all. Later, when Major cross-examined Officer King, he asked him whether *he* knew in advance the mob was coming. King was frank and brief. "Yes." Even the out-of-town reporters caught the implication: Sheriff Brown knew what was coming; he *chose* not to act.

At one point during cross-examination, Major asked Brown to confirm that the negro taken from the jail was the one Regina Almstedt had identified as her attacker. Hulen was on his feet objecting before Brown could answer. This time Judge Gantt sent the jurors out of the courtroom, and the lawyers assembled in front of his desk for an argument loud enough to be heard by the spectators. Major, Harris, and Starrett argued that Barkwell had been arbitrarily singled out and charged with premeditated murder. To counter the accusation of premeditation, they needed to show the jury that he was surrounded by hundreds of citizens enraged by a heinous crime. Davis and Hulen argued that the supposed crime of James Scott was irrelevant and that the defense was referring to it only to inflame the passions of the jury. Whatever Scott had or hadn't done, the jury needed to focus on *Barkwell's* behavior. After ten minutes of debate, Judge Gantt sustained Hulen's objection.

Now Hulen came to his most important witnesses, a trio of young reporters. First came 23-year-old Francis Misselwitz, who had graduated from the University's journalism school the year before and had taken a job with the St. Louis *Post-Dispatch*. Alerted to the possibility of a lynching, he had arrived on the 6:15 train on the night of April 28th, noticed nothing unusual downtown, and decided to wait for developments in the comfort of a pool hall. At about 11:00 someone came to the door to announce that the lynching was on. Misselwitz hurried to the jail in time to see the mob burn off the last hinge of the hallway door. The faces of the mob's leaders, he wrote in a by-lined story, had been "cast in bold relief by the torchlight." After the crowd started to the bridge, Misselwitz rode there in an automobile, arriving in time to follow Hermann Almstedt to the center of the mob. Soon he was standing under the arc-light, close enough to ask Scott questions and to record his every word and gesture. "A big man," Misselwitz wrote in his story, "elbowed his way to the negro, and, in silence, placed a one-inch noose over his head." Misselwitz watched the big man work methodically, tying the loose end of the rope to the bridge rail, lifting him onto the railing, and shoving him over with both hands. Then, Misselwitz wrote, "The big man ducked into the crowd. I have not seen him since." The implication seemed to be that if he *had* seen him again, he would have recognized him.

Misselwitz should have been an ideal witness. On the stand, he recalled in great detail James Scott's prayers and his insistence that it was Ollie Watson who had attacked Regina Almstedt. He remembered Scott's saying that Watson had shaved three times in two days at the jailhouse. He remembered Scott's lifting his chin to show where Watson's neck had been cut by the girl's umbrella. Misselwitz's testimony produced details of this kind in abundance, but when Hulen asked if the man who had put a noose around James Scott's neck was the defendant, the young reporter balked. Well, he had really only seen the man's back. The man was the same size and build as the defendant, but he couldn't identify him as George Barkwell.

Misselwitz had a good deal on his mind that summer, some of which may have cooled his enthusiasm for denouncing a well-connected Columbian. Soon after his lynching story appeared, he had been surprised by a phone call from Walter Williams. Williams had said flattering things about his work and his potential for a fine career, and had offered him a faculty job at the Journalism School in Columbia. The paperwork was still being processed. The backing of Walter Williams could do an ambitious young man a world of good—if that young man did nothing to alienate the leading men in the community where he hoped to launch his career.

Charles Nutter, the next witness, was a 20-year-old journalism student whose size invited Barkwell sympathizers to whisper *pipsqueak* to their neighbors. He had left the family farm at sixteen and moved to Columbia on his own, working for two years to save the tuition he needed to enroll. On the night of the lynching, he had stuck to the mob's leaders like a shadow and accompanied Scott the whole length of the march down to Stewart Bridge. At the bridge, he told the jury,

> I was standing in front of Misselwitz, right next to
> Scott. I would talk to him and then remonstrate with
> the crowd. Scott was calm and coolly protested his
> innocence. He prayed, and his prayer was the
> outbreathing of a spirit absolutely innocent. Then he
> charged Ollie Watson, a negro who was confined in the
> same cell with him as having committed the crime and
> as having confessed to him ... . Then the defendant,
> George Barkwell, came rushing in with a one-inch
> rope. I saw George Barkwell put the rope around
> Scott's neck, lift him to the railing of the bridge and

> push him over. I looked down and saw his body clear
> of the ground and hurried away.

Hulen asked Nutter to clarify his location relative to Barkwell. "I was right against him," Nutter replied. To reach Scott, Barkwell had pushed him back into Misselwitz's chest.

On cross-examination, Congressman Major went at Nutter as if he were attempting to pry open an oyster. Did the young man even know George Barkwell's name prior that the evening of the lynching? No, he didn't. Could the young man describe the clothing the man with the rope had worn that evening? No, he couldn't. If it was too dark to see the clothing, how could Nutter be so confident about the identity of the man he saw? It wasn't too dark, the moonlight and the arc-light made everything clear. He had seen Barkwell's face at the jail and heard him called George then. When he saw the face again at the bridge, he recognized it, and when he heard a bystander call him Barkwell, he double-checked the first and last name with a man standing nearby. Barkwell had been in shirtsleeves; he hadn't studied the clothing more closely because it didn't seem important.

Well, Congressman Major wondered aloud, *if Nutter was so very sure that Barkwell was the man who had hanged Scott, why hadn't he reported that fact in the* Missourian? *Wouldn't that have been an important element of the story?* Because, Nutter answered, Barkwell might have sued the paper for libel. *But*, Congressman Major replied, *truth is an absolute defense in a case of libel. A truthful reporter should have nothing to fear*. Perhaps, replied Nutter, but naming names in a story of this kind just isn't done. *Well, then, why didn't Nutter give Barkwell's name to the police the night of the lynching rather than wait for the grand jury investigation?* He *had* reported the name that very night, at Boone Tavern, to Officer Pleas King.

Hulen called Foster Hailey, another journalism student. Hailey, an angular 22-year-old Navy veteran, did the most acrobatic reporting on the evening of the lynching. The cells in the county jail were cages barred on all sides and on top. Before the mob reached Scott's cell, Hailey climbed up one side of it and stationed himself on top, where he could hear everything and see whatever the light allowed. He had seen Barkwell peer into Scott's cell and say, "I think he's in here!" He had heard the Sheriff and others address Barkwell by name. A few minutes into the assault on the cell, "the flame of the torch went out, and I saw Barkwell monkeying with the tank a little bit. The flame came back and the two men who were burning their way into Scott's cell went on with their work."

"*Monkeying* with the gas tank!" Congressman Major snorted during cross-examination. Just what did young Hailey mean by *monkeying*? Had he seen exactly what the man he supposed to be Barkwell had done with the acetylene tank? No, Hailey had to admit, he hadn't. If people wanted to believe that Barkwell had chosen that moment to check the address of the manufacturer, Foster Hailey could say nothing to dissuade them.

THE FIRST witness for the defense was Emmett Smith, chief cashier at the Exchange National Bank. Smith was one of the best-liked men in Columbia: treasurer of the Commercial Club and the Rotary Club, former Exalted Ruler of the

Elks. In manner and appearance, he was a striking contrast to the thin, intense undergraduates who had just left the stand. Middle-aged, comfortably round, with fat cheeks and a tiny bow of a smile, he was upbeat and droll. He often told people that he had attended the University for a year "until I got too wise and quit." He had been elected the county's Public Administrator, he would say with a smile, "in spite of Democratic affiliations in politics." He belonged to the country club, though (unlike Frank Harris here) he didn't have all day to devote to golf. Everything about Smith suggested that he enjoyed life. Even on the witness stand, some of his comments made people laugh.

Senator Harris asked him if he had been on Stewart Bridge the night of the lynching and if he had seen George Barkwell. Yes, indeed, he had seen George there. He had found his friend standing on the north side of the bridge, clear across the roadway from Scott, and had talked for several minutes with him and Pierce Neidermeyer while some other men readied the negro for hanging. They were still talking when a cry of "There he goes!" went up from the men on the south side, who scattered in all directions. He, Barkwell and Neidermeyer stayed to chat a bit longer.

Senator Harris called Pierce Neidermeyer, a young man from a socially prominent family. He testified that he had seen George Barkwell on the courthouse lawn, standing in front of the mob with his hand raised to stop the march to Stewart Bridge. Neidermeyer had heard him urging the men to wait to hear from someone's father. He testified that he followed the crowd to the bridge and had been talking with Barkwell and Emmett Smith for "about five minutes" when Scott was thrown from the other side of the bridge. He remembered distinctly that Barkwell had grasped his arm and lifted him slightly as both men stood on tiptoe to see what was happening.

Hulen now saw clearly which way the wind was blowing. On cross-examination, he asked Neidermeyer when he had found a chance to talk with Barkwell after the lynching. Neidermeyer said they had happened to meet on the street. And what had they talked about? Hulen asked. "He asked if I remembered seeing him at the lynching." Hulen didn't mention certain legal terms that must have been passing through his head, terms like *perjury* and *subornation thereto*.

Harris called Roy McDonald, a clerk for the MKT railroad, who said that he had seen Barkwell on the bridge that evening. Barkwell was talking with Emmett Smith on the north side of the bridge. McDonald kept them in sight as he waded through the crowd for five to ten minutes to join them. He was standing right beside Barkwell, at least 30 feet from Scott, when the man was thrown over the bridge. Other witnesses followed, but the heart of the defense was the testimony of Smith, Neidermeyer, and McDonald, which interlocked so seamlessly that there was no assailing it. By the time court recessed on Wednesday evening, Barkwell's supporters were organizing a dinner to celebrate the victory they were confident would come the next day.

The next morning, after a night of thunderstorms, the courtroom was again packed with spectators. Senator Harris called Hollis Edwards, city editor of the Columbia *Daily Tribune*, as his first witness. Harris held up a newspaper for Edwards and the jury to see: the *Tribune* from April 27th.

He asked Edwards if he had written the lead story about Regina Almstedt's identification of Scott as her attacker. Edwards' "yes" beat Hulen's objection by a split second. Gantt sustained the objection.

Harris held up the editorial page from April 28 and asked who had written the editorial. Hulen objected and was sustained.

Harris held up the front page from April 28 and pointed to the article reporting that "men of sound judgment" agreed that "taxpayers should be saved any costs that might accrue from a trial" of James Scott. Who had written this article? Hulen was on his feet now, objecting vociferously. Judge Gantt quieted the courtroom, sent the jury out, and asked lawyers for both sides to approach the bench.

The lawyers hissed at each other for several minutes, their words indistinct to the spectators. Having heard what each side was trying to accomplish, Judge Gantt offered a compromise. The defense could ask Edwards one more question along these lines, but not in front of the jury. The question and answer would be stricken from the record before the jury returned. If the defense insisted on playing this matter to the gallery, Gantt wanted to get it over with quickly. The lawyers resumed their positions. Harris pointed to the article again and asked his one question, "Who provided you with information for this article?" Edwards named three names: Chief Rowland, Sheriff Brown, and Prosecutor Hulen.

The final witness for the defense was, indirectly, Hulen himself. Senator Harris asked Judge Gantt's permission to read aloud the charge that the Prosecutor had filed against James Scott the morning before the lynching. Hulen couldn't object, since he had introduced the document into the record himself. Addressing the gallery as well as the jury, Harris read slowly and emphatically. "Now comes the prosecuting attorney for the state and files his information charging the defendant with the crime of rape."

GEORGE STARRETT began the most effective of the defense's summations by saying that he did not believe it was necessary for him to ask the gentlemen of the jury to stand by the oaths they had taken. He believed the jury honest, and to remind them of their duty would seem to mean that he distrusted them. Their duty was to render a verdict according to the evidence. Mr. Davis seemed sometimes to forget this when he talked about "sending a message to the state" by convicting George Barkwell. Starrett was sure that the jury would not convict an innocent man in order to send a message on behalf of Mr. Davis.

Columbia, Starrett told the jury, had lived in peace and equanimity for years until the day of April 20, when a "fiendish crime" was committed and "a white girl was ravished and despoiled." This brought Hulen to his feet, objecting that Starrett's line of argument was uncalled for, and that he was insinuating that James Scott was guilty of a crime for which he had never come to trial. Judge Gantt overruled, saying that he did not understand this to be Starrett's point.

Starrett then reminded the jury forcefully of the charge Hulen had made against Scott. "Now comes the prosecuting attorney for the state and files his information for the crime of rape." A prosecuting attorney is bound by his oath of office to present only charges he believes to be true, Starrett

105

explained. An honest man wouldn't bring this charge unless he knew it was true.

Now, was George Barkwell present on the night James Scott was lynched? Yes, Starrett said, he was there, along with hundreds of other spectators. Because Barkwell was present at the jail and at the bridge, Ruby Hulen and Henry Davis had picked him as a man they could charge with first-degree murder. They had no case against him. "The sheriff and the probate judge say he did nothing. All that George Barkwell did was what the sheriff had been asking every man there to do—to plead with the mob. A boy has testified that he was 'monkeying' with the torch, but there is no evidence to show that he did anything but 'monkey' with it."

Another young fellow, Charles Nutter, testified that George Barkwell put a rope around the negro's neck and threw him from the bridge. "Gentlemen, somebody has lied. Now who is it? Who is Nutter? Who is Hailey?" They were ciphers to the town. "This man Nutter is one of these newspaper reporters who is always going around after news. All of them feed on publicity. I do not believe a word of what Nutter said. If you are to believe him, you have to call W. E. Smith, one of our best citizens, a liar." Starrett delivered a stirring encomium on Emmett Smith's character and his service to the community. Everyone knew what a reliable man Smith was. "I'd rather believe a man I *know* rather than a man I *don't know*. I'd rather believe W. E. Smith than a whole *basketful* of Nutters."

By the time Ruby Hulen began the final summation for the prosecution, the spectators had listened to four long speeches and the early risers among them were hungry for lunch. Hulen began by expressing resentment that the lawyers for the defense claimed he was prosecuting Barkwell to make a point. He was prosecuting this case because it was his duty to do so, because Barkwell had been indicted on the basis of credible evidence. Lawyers for the defense apparently had odd notions of duty. Congressman Major, for instance, "your representative who draws $17,500 per year for being in Washington, D.C." felt comfortable setting those duties aside to spend time in Columbia defending George Barkwell.

Major objected strenuously. If Hulen didn't know that Congress was in recess, he told Judge Gantt, the jury surely did, but he wanted Hulen to stop casting unfounded aspersions. "Then I withdraw the comment," said Hulen, and moved on, summarizing the case against Barkwell and emphasizing the testimony of Charles Nutter. He mentioned the savage attacks of Major, Harris, and Starrett against the young man's character.

According to the less-than-reliable *Tribune*, he then—astonishingly—asked the jury to consider that "somewhere, Nutter probably has a father who believes in his truthfulness." This could have been entirely mischievous reporting on the *Tribune's* part. If Hulen said such a thing, he must have wanted the jury to remember that, high above this scene of hatred, cravenness, and duplicity, Nutter had a *Father* who recognized his truthfulness.

The jury was out for 11 minutes. After the verdict was read, Barkwell was mobbed by well-wishers, who eventually formed a long line waiting to shake his hand and congratulate him. Davis and Hulen withdrew to the Prosecutor's office and issued a statement saying that the very fact the case had come to trial was a vindication of the rule of law. Then Hulen went immediately to the office of the Circuit Court and suspended action against all other defendants in the James Scott case.

That evening, groups of Barkwell supporters walked up and down Broadway, singing and laughing. They developed a cheer of sorts. Call: "Isn't George Barkwell ALL RIGHT?" Response: "George Barkwell is ALL RIGHT!" Rumors were heard all over town that a mob was coming after Charles Nutter to give him the thrashing of his life. Nutter and some of his friends reacted by walking the sidewalks themselves, listening to the threats and the shouts of derision. The next day Nutter packed a bag and bought a round-trip ticket to St. Louis on the 1:00 a.m. train. He would be back in two weeks, he said. A group of journalist friends walked him to the Wabash station, stopping along the way to buy cigarettes in a restaurant. As they passed through the door, every customer swiveled in his chair to stare at Nutter in silence. The proprietor came to the counter and sold the cigarettes without saying a word. When Nutter turned to leave, the shouting started:

"There goes the son of a bitch!"

"Let's get the state's star witness!"

"Hit him!"

Nutter kept walking, picked up his suitcase at a nearby hotel, and boarded his train.

Ollie Watson's trial for the rape of Ernestine Huggard began eleven days after Barkwell's acquittal. The trial was in Mexico, so Judge Gantt presided in his own courtroom. Ruby Hulen led the prosecution, George Starrett the defense. Just before the trial began, a reporter asked Hulen if he intended to charge Watson with the assault on Regina Almstedt. "It's according to how this case comes out," he replied. He was asking for the death penalty in the Huggard case.

The two-day trial proceeded smoothly to a conviction. The jury agreed on the first ballot that Watson was guilty, but struggled for nearly an hour with the sentence. In the end, they gave him twenty-four years. Watson glanced nervously around the courtroom during his sentencing. When Judge Gantt asked if he had something he wanted to say, he begged to be locked away immediately.

The Boone County Courthouse

Watching the Watchers

... the historic tradition that the police are the public and the public are the police....

—Sir Robert Peel

The Police Academy

I could claim—it wouldn't be an outright lie—that a sense of civic duty compelled me to enroll in the Citizens' Police Academy. But the aimless curiosity of middle age had a deal to do with it. My day job had grown routine. Ten weeks of evening classes covering "every aspect of police work" wasn't a trip to Machu Picchu or Tibet, but it would give me something fresh to think about. I obviously couldn't have anticipated that the Mercury Merrick case was coming my way.

I assumed that the Academy would be an exercise in public relations, with the sharp corners of police work carefully rounded off. Almost immediately, however, we were introduced to Sergeant Ken Smith, the Department's specialist in the use of force. Smith, a former paratrooper and intelligence officer, was not disposed to soft-peddle anything. He had a black belt in karate and a list of certifications as a weapons expert. His résumé included courses like "Chemical Munitions" and "Counter Terrorism and Hostage Rescue"—much of this training done on his own time and at his own expense. He had been a policeman for 28 years, and had never held a strictly civilian job. I've seldom met a man keener about his work.

Earlier in his career, he had faced three "lethal force situations," meaning, he explained, that three men had tried to kill him. One wrestled him to the ground, took away his pistol, rammed it under his bulletproof vest, and pulled the trigger. A misfire. Smith recovered the pistol, racked it to clear the jammed round, and made the arrest. As he told the story, a smile unzipped at one corner of his mouth. He was 53 years old now, his hair white and thinning, his chest flattened and his stomach rounded. Policemen generally retire by his age, collecting good pensions after twenty years of service. He had stayed on, becoming a shift supervisor and a trainer.

Smith gave the Citizens—most of us his age or older— two hours of instruction in "hard-hand" tactics. First we observed demonstrations of "fire arms retention and recovery." With an officer named Bennett playing the hapless villain, Smith taught us how to beat away the arm of a bad guy reaching for our holster, how to disarm a pistol-wielding assailant with a scissor-strike to the wrist and hand, how to free ourselves in a hostage situation by twisting suddenly and slapping away a pistol held to the back of our heads. The rubber gun flew from Officer Bennett's hand, bouncing off a desk, off the floor. Bennett, who had been involved in two lethal force situations himself, was taking quite a beating. He complained good-humoredly about bruises he'd suffered in past demonstrations.

Smith moved on to "pressure point control tactics." He approached Bennett from behind and hooked a finger under the angle of his jaw. Bennett went limp with pain. Smith backed him effortlessly across the room: "So if you're a bystander, and I have to arrest this guy, does this look like police brutality? Not at all."

He told Bennett to try to strangle him. Bennett obeyed, and as he did, Smith intercepted one of his friend's hands. He applied excruciating pressure near the base of Bennett's thumb, twisted Bennett's arms behind him, cuffed him, and raised the cuffed hands high as he pushed him toward an imaginary police car. (I later learned that Smith had used this arm-twisting and cuffing technique twenty years earlier while arresting a woman who had made the mistake of spilling a milkshake on his wife. He had executed the maneuver with enough gusto to fracture one of the woman's wrists in the process.)

Now we had our own chance to inflict pain. Following Smith's instructions, we rested an index finger on our upper lips as if we were children pretending to have mustaches. Then, on Smith's signal, we pushed up against the septum of the nose with our knuckles. At first I felt only a mild discomfort, but I was a determined student. I increased the pressure until suddenly I felt it—a jolt that brought tears to my eyes. For days afterwards I would gently test the bruise with my fingertip while I sat at my desk.

THE CITIZENS' Academy was largely a lecture course, but there were practical sessions, including some of the firearm training given to authentic police recruits. So, early the next Saturday morning, I reported to a training facility at the edge of town, where Officer Bennett issued me a virtual pistol and a virtual can of mace. Bennett showed me how to rack the pistol and asked me to aim it out a window. I held the gun at arm's length in one hand as I had done with my cap gun fifty years earlier. Bennett laughed and shook his head: "Two hands. Two hands. Like this." He sent me into the training room, where Sergeant Smith was waiting.

Smith told me that the first scenario would involve a routine traffic stop. He positioned me in front of a huge movie screen and started the projector. A car in front of me pulled over and my virtual partner, who materialized unannounced, told me to wait in our squad car while he walked up to talk to the driver. Just before he reached the car, its backup lights flashed and its tires squealed. My partner stiff-armed an approaching taillight and fell, gingerly, on the edge of the road. The suspect car stopped, then started forward. I raised my laser pistol and shouted as loudly as my nature allows: "Halt! Step out of the vehicle!"

Astonishingly, it seemed to work. The door opened and a man spun out, pulling something from his hip pocket as he turned. I was firing, and so was he. He went down on the concrete—hard. A first-rate fall, much better than my partner's. Perhaps he was a faculty member from the University theater department, I thought. I lowered my pistol to have a look.

The lights came up, and Sergeant Smith asked in a flat voice that expressed no curiosity, "Why did you shoot him?"

I hesitated. "Because I saw his gun." It was as much a question as an answer.

"No," said Sergeant Smith, "You fired your first shot before it was possible for you to see the gun." He ran a slow-motion replay. This time my point of aim showed on the screen as a white X inside a circle. The X floated near the car door as the man opened it. It didn't quite keep up with him as he swung out and pivoted. My first shot glowed green between him and the car—a miss.

Sergeant Smith froze this frame. He was right. The man's hand was still behind his hip. I found this an opportune time to mention the curious connections among expectation, perception, and memory. How we sometimes remember events as happening in ways we only hoped or feared they would happen. "Uh-huh," answered Sergeant Smith.

The film advanced slowly, pausing at each of my shots. The man's hand came up with a dark object in it, indistinct on the grainy film. It could have been a wallet flapping open, a paintbrush, or an extra-crispy drumstick. The hand was just dropping to aim when my second shot flashed. A yellow spot—a non-lethal hit—appeared on the man's left shoulder. His pistol flashed back twice, the second flash simultaneous with my third shot. A red dot covered most of his forehead.

But it was the first shot Sergeant Smith wanted me to think about. "Now you'll have to explain that shot in court, won't you? You'll have to explain that to Geraldo Rivera." Geraldo came up often in Sergeant Smith's conversation. "You know how Geraldo got his start, don't you? Doing stories on police brutality. Saying that policemen are the real criminals. Second-guessing policemen when they were there and he wasn't. That's why I never second-guess an officer."

Forty minutes into my firearms session, Sergeant Smith told me to relax and wipe down my palms. We were about to begin the eighth and final scenario. Actually, my palms were dry, but my left hand kept testing the bruised septum of my nose. I'd been doing well, I thought, in scenarios with bank robbers, fugitives, domestic beatings, and stabbings. I'd have given myself a C+. What Sergeant Smith would have given me I'll never know. Between scenarios he pointed out my errors and reviewed any shots I had fired. Then he continued his monologue about Geraldo Rivera, plaintiff's lawyers, and the inability of the public to understand the pressures of police work. "They expect a police officer to be perfect, every time. And they've never been there." He disliked the idea of civilian boards of inquiry, he said. They were certainly unnecessary in Columbia, Missouri, our home town, where he *personally* reviewed every incident in which an officer used a firearm.

On his signal, I loaded and racked my laser Glock. He started the projector. The dispatcher told me that there was a report of a drunk in an alley carrying a baby. He had dropped the baby a couple of times already. I waited for a few seconds, realizing that I was standing as a virtual policeman in a place I had often stood as an actual civilian, an alley just north of Broadway.

A Hispanic man with a mustache staggered around a corner, carrying an infant car seat with a life-sized doll in it. I tried a medium-loud voice: "Sir, please stop and set the child down softly! Let's keep everyone safe." He acted as if he hadn't heard or understood. Perhaps he knew no English. I knew no Spanish. He kept zigzagging toward me. "Sir! Please stand where you are! Put the child down! Softly." He took a few more steps toward me and pulled a machete from behind the baby seat. Now he looked like an extra from a pirate movie.

I raised my pistol and shouted commands. He staggered toward me with the machete waving overhead. I remembered the canister of laser mace stuffed into my jeans pocket, and soon I had both hands loaded and aimed. "Stop, or I will have to spray you!" Now I had to hope that he *didn't* understand English. He kept coming, and when he was just beyond arm's length I gave the canister one tap. A small white cloud appeared right on the man's nose. The projector stopped and the lights came on. Sergeant Smith asked me if I had used my mace. Had he been sleeping? "Yes, I did."

"Well, then, you killed the baby. Babies are mouth breathers. They suck the mace into their lungs, which are undeveloped. It kills them. You should have gone for a head shot. The baby was in a child safety seat. It would have absorbed the impact of another fall."

Now my palms may have been sweating. I thought about how tiny the spot of mace was, how exactly on the nose, but that seemed a feeble argument. A head shot, though? I pointed out that if the car seat was adequate protection, then the child wasn't in immediate danger, and I could have just kept out of the man's reach. "If I fire, I may hit the child rather than the man. If I keep retreating, no one is hurt. Why take a chance?"

Sergeant Smith was clearly scoring this as a wrong answer. "Right, and we have citizens looking out their windows watching an armed policeman being chased down an alley by a man with a baby in his arms! *Nossir!*"

Sergeant Smith didn't replay this scenario, though I would have liked for him to see the commendable accuracy of that left-handed burst of mace. I didn't like breaking off the session with a dead baby on my conscience. But time was up, the next Citizen was waiting her turn, and I knew it would be fruitless to second-guess the sergeant.

SOON AFTER we received our firearms training, we met Captain Zim Schwartze, an athletic woman about forty years old whose energy seemed to flow all the way to the spikes of her blonde hair. There were rumors that she had joined the department after a successful run on *American Gladiator*. In truth, she had joined after she wearied of her work as an industrial engineer. Police work suited her better. She rose quickly through the ranks and was now in charge of the East District—nearly half of the total force. If Sergeant Smith had shown us the yang of policing, Captain Schwartze was about to show us its yin. Her personal hero, she told us, wasn't Wyatt Earp. It was Sir Robert Peel.

Peel was the British Home Secretary in the 1820s, when criminal gangs terrorized London. The professional policemen of the time were gaudily uniformed men armed with cutlasses, pistols, and carbines. Night and day they sallied out of their station houses in squads to make arrests. The result was unsatisfactory. The penitentiaries were packed with gangsters, but they produced little penitence. They became schools for thugs, operated at public expense.

Hanging criminals was comparatively thrifty and efficient, and for a time England hanged them at a higher rate, for more trivial crimes, than any other nation in the world. The philanthropic side of the British character, however, wouldn't tolerate enough hangings to reduce the criminal population by brute subtraction.

Robert Peel, Captain Schwartze informed us, was a genius. He saw that law enforcement was paying too much attention to hardened criminals and too little to average citizens, who naturally wanted peace and good order in their neighborhoods. Peel envisioned a new kind of policeman who could work with these ordinary citizens to tame the disorderly city. His policemen would dress almost like civilian gentlemen. They would go into the city unarmed except for a baton that served as a symbol of their office. These New Police—soon nicknamed Peelers or Bobbies— were to be assigned short beats that they could walk four times an hour, every hour, visible encouragements to good order. They were to familiarize themselves with every street, courtyard, alley, house, and outbuilding on the beat. They were to become acquainted, if possible, with every resident. They were to spend their shift talking with the civilians they met, not with other policemen. The keynote of Peel's philosophy appeared as a PowerPoint slide in Captain Schwartze's presentation:

> The police at all times should maintain a relationship with the public that gives reality to the historic tradition that the police are the public and the public are the police; the police are the only members of the public who are paid to give their full-time attention to duties which are incumbent on every citizen in the interest of community welfare.

Peel and his police commissioners allowed the Bobbies great latitude in deciding what duties were incumbent on them. If an officer felt that he could serve best on a given day by helping a mother search for her lost child, the commissioners approved. If he decided to help a parent discipline a rebellious daughter by pretending that he was about to arrest her, they approved. If he decided that he would knock every morning on the door of a man who might otherwise oversleep and lose his job, fine. The job of the policeman wasn't primarily to respond to crime, but to prevent it.

As I heard Zim Schwartze translate Peel's vision into contemporary terms, I began to hope I was listening to Columbia's next police chief:

"Police officers tend to be competitive, action-oriented individuals. In traditional policing, they focus on the bad guys and see nothing else. You go into a neighborhood to make an arrest. The neighbors turn out. They are curious. The traditional police officer tries to drive them back indoors. *Police business*, he says, and tells them to go home. This makes them nervous and suspicious. It's a neighbor who is being arrested, after all. Soon the officer is having to call for backup to control the crowd. That's how a riot might start. When a community-oriented officer goes into that situation, he turns to the neighbors and says, *Look, I need your help. I need to take Jimmy to the station. He'll be upset and frightened about this. Can any of you find a relative to help him stay calm? Is his grandma around? His uncle?*

"Pay attention to the law-abiding citizens. Get them involved. You could spend your whole shift in your car answering 911 calls, but get out of the car every once in a while. Talk to the people on your beat. Ask them what you can do to help them. Ask them where the problems are."

READING ABOUT Robert Peel wasn't the only thing that encouraged Captain Schwartze's interest in community-oriented policing. She joined the force soon after a policing catastrophe, to which she alluded without flinching or elaborating.

Kim Linzie, granddaughter of a Methodist minister and daughter of a Vietnam veteran, grew up in a black neighborhood that was sometimes patrolled by officers in helmets moving in formation. The police made her nervous, and her unhappy life soon began to follow a pattern that would make it almost inevitable that she would have to deal with them. She left school at age fifteen; she worked at Taco Bell and drank heavily. Her first arrest came in October of 1984, when she was a 19-year-old sitting drunk at dawn in a car she had backed into a telephone pole. Two squad cars stopped, bottling the car in, and the officers got out to talk to her. Linzie panicked. She gunned the engine and ploughed though a gap between the cruisers, denting both. For a few blocks, through a red light and past a stop sign, she stayed ahead of the police. Then she ran her car into a ditch and took off on foot. At 5'1" and 100 pounds, she wasn't a powerful sprinter. She made it half a block. The sentence was five years of probation.

Soon after, Linzie moved into a rental house two blocks from her parole office. One of her roommates owned a Mercury Bobcat she was willing to share. Linzie bought a stereo for the car, helped with the payments, and had her own key. But the Bobcat became a source of friction between the girls. About 2:30 on the afternoon of July 3, 1985, they were inside it arguing so loudly that they drew the attention of officers in a passing patrol car. The officers found Linzie at the wheel and the roommate in the back seat, throwing Linzie's belongings out onto the pavement. Linzie's parole officer appeared and said that he could handle the situation, so the police officers, who were at the end of their shift, went back to the station.

Through the Bobcat's lowered window the parole officer noticed the smell of beer in the car. He persuaded Linzie to pull into the parole office parking lot, and the roommate went inside to call her mother. When the roommate returned, she announced that if Linzie drove the car away, she was going to call the police and report it as stolen. The parole officer urged Linzie to give up the car. Linzie said she wouldn't. What she would do, she said, was drive it to a park, clear her head, and be back at 4:15 for a scheduled parole meeting. She drove off, and the roommate called the police.

The call went out to a fresh shift of patrol officers who knew nothing about what had happened earlier in the afternoon. An officer in a cruiser attempted to pull her over only a few minutes later. She kept driving at the speed limit. More cruisers joined in, attempting unsuccessfully to pull in front of her and cut her off. She headed east on Broadway with five patrol cars buzzing around her. At the intersection of William Street, a civilian car had stopped for a red light. Linzie couldn't get past it, and she came to a stop with cruisers on every side. Four of the five officers got out of their cars. One braced himself on the hood of his cruiser, aiming his pistol through the Bobcat's passenger window. Linzie panicked, backed up into the patrol car behind her, rammed the civilian car in front of her, backed into the patrol car again, and paused for a few seconds. An officer approached from the rear, another from the driver's side, a third from the front—all with pistols drawn. Linzie drove forward, trying to squeeze the Bobcat between the civilian car and a patrol car. A female officer was pounding on her windshield with a pistol butt. Other officers were pounding at other windows. Linzie pressed the accelerator to the floor. The female officer, apparently pinned against the side of her cruiser, fell from view, and the shooting began.

After Linzie's funeral the following Sunday, 250 people marched on the police station carrying signs demanding an investigation. How could a spat between roommates result in the police killing an unarmed 19-year-old girl? Wasn't this a racist shooting? A week after the funeral, a mob in the Douglass Park area began throwing rocks at passing cars. Soon they had shut down Providence Road, a principal north-south artery in Columbia. The police got their first call about 1:00 a.m. No patrol cars appeared. The mob held the street for ninety minutes before the police called leaders of the black community and asked them to come out of their homes and deal with their young people.

When Captain Schwartze took command of the officers on Columbia's East District, she delivered them a lecture that must have caused some head-scratching. "What do you consider a great shift? Maybe you answer fifteen calls, stop ten cars, issue some tickets, make a couple of arrests. That would be a great shift. But if in the process of doing all that you make the police ten enemies, *don't expect me to congratulate you*. Without the goodwill of the citizens, we can't do our jobs. Policemen don't see crimes committed; citizens do."

Schwartze told her officers that preventative community policing required them to treat citizens courteously—even citizens who are also criminals. But it didn't mean, as some of them seemed to fear, "kissing babies and shaking hands," and didn't mean being soft on crime. In fact, it meant being harder on crime, even the smallest matters. Violations of zoning ordinances and building codes, improper disposal of trash, music loud enough to annoy the neighbors, the pettiest of vandalism—none of this would be tolerated by an officer who wanted to encourage good order on his or her beat. She told stories about her own time patrolling a tough neighborhood. One night she was driving her cruiser down a one-way street when she saw a bicycle with no lights approaching from the opposite direction. She wasn't going to let this go uncorrected. She turned on her light bar and tapped her siren. The rider jumped off his bicycle and started off across a lawn.

Officer Schwartze jumped out of her car and gave chase. The bicyclist was young and fast, but—as she says—not especially bright: he held on to his handlebars as he ran. They raced across lawns and lots for a few blocks and the man reached Douglass Park before she was able to tackle him. At that point, wrestling in the grass, they started to pummel each other. "He was pounding on me and I was pounding on him," she says, when another officer joined in and got the man cuffed. After the cuffs went on, Captain Schwartze says, "We chatted. I explained what he had done wrong. The guy says to me, 'If you're going to do that to me for not having a bicycle light, what are you going to do if I do something really serious?'"

This, for Captain Schwartze, was the payoff line. When she delivered it, she looked like a teacher who had finally cornered a student into seeing the point. She then added, as an afterthought, that the bicyclist had a pocket full of crack cocaine.

She liked to tell the story of putting on her civilian clothes one evening and joining a group of citizens from her beat on National Night Out. They marched through the neighborhood to show that they intended to take the streets back from the prostitutes and the dope peddlers, and they ended the march in front of the house of a notorious crack dealer. There, after some sign-waving and cheering, the crowd began to melt away. Eventually only two of them were left, Zim Schwartze and Wynna Faye Elbert, a blonde woman about thirty-five and a black woman about fifty. From the dark house came a man's voice, loud and threatening. "You bitches better clear out of here. This street is mine."

Schwartze says she wanted to run for cover. She was not in body armor, not armed, far from a radio or a phone. The man was surely armed, perhaps high, and very angry. "We're going to die," I thought. "We're going to die right here." But Elbert wasn't about to move, and Schwartze wasn't about to leave her alone. Elbert looked up at the house and shouted back, "No, *you're* gonna clear out. This street is *mine*."

TOWARD THE end of the Academy, each of the Citizens had an opportunity to ride with an officer on patrol. I rode on a Friday night with Jeff Rukstad, a 28-year-old who had joined the city's force four months earlier. As a newcomer, he hadn't a chance of drawing a day shift, and he wanted to spend evenings with his wife and 5-year-old son, so the night shift was inevitable. On weekdays he slept while his wife worked and his son was in day care. On weekends he slept very little: His son tried to keep quiet, but couldn't, unless he was napping beside dad. Rukstad missed sleeping with his wife, he said, and his doctor was concerned about his diet, but he loved his job.

We were just out of the station when Rukstad claimed one of three unanswered calls stacked at the bottom of the dispatch screen. It was a peace disturbance three miles south of us at the intersection of Providence Road and Nifong Boulevard. The area is one of those depressing edge pieces of Columbia that might just as well be a depressing edge piece of Boston or Albuquerque: big franchise stores, houses and apartments in neutral colors, empty sidewalks and wide streets. As he swept down Providence with his light bar flashing, Rukstad got more information from the radio and from his laptop. The call, he said, had come from the manager of the SoCo Club, "an alternative life-style bar." A customer was making a ruckus and refusing to leave. No, the dispatcher added, now the customer had left, hurried no doubt by the phone call. But the manager was concerned that she might create problems for other businesses in the area. She was a white woman about thirty wearing khakis and a short white jacket with patches of brown. She might be walking over to the Break Time in the next block to call for a ride home.

Officer Rukstad spotted her just before she reached the convenience store. He turned left to intercept her, hitting the siren briefly as he turned. She stopped immediately, blinking in surprise. She was under a streetlight, standing on a tiny island of grass surrounded by concrete. Faces in passing cars were turning to watch the scene. She was drunk enough to slow her speech, but nowhere near staggering. I had been this drunk myself, though not for years, and I suspected that Jeff Rukstad had, too. He called in his location, then stepped up to the woman and asked, "What happened back there?"

"Nothing," she answered, sounding like a truculent teenager. She took a breath. "Don't do this to me," she pleaded. "I was just going to call for a ride home. Don't do this to me!"

"I'm not doing anything to you," Rukstad answered, a thin note of irritation in his voice. "I just asked what happened back there. Can I see your license?"

The woman opened her wallet and tried to hand it to the officer. He wouldn't take the whole wallet. "Could you take out just the license, please?"

Back in the car, he typed in the license number into his computer and got a screen topped by the woman's name and the label SHOPLIFTER. The page was full of incident reports. Catherine had two arrests for shoplifting and three or four for domestic abuse of an adult. Her license had been revoked for driving under the influence. There were a few reports listing her as a victim and few others where she just seems to have been on the scene. Once she had been placed in protective custody. It took Officer Rukstad a couple of minutes to learn this much and to radio Joint Communications, which checked for more recent violations and outstanding warrants. Catherine waited under the street light in the cool night air, watching people in passing cars turn their heads to look at her. Rukstad stepped out again.

"Where are you going, Catherine?"

"I was just going to call for a ride home."

"I can give you a ride home. Where do you live?"

She named her street, a one-block cul-de-sac sandwiched between parks. Catherine was the neighbor of one of my friends, who told me later that the last house on the block had just become "some sort of halfway house for women with drug and alcohol problems." Catherine said she believed she'd just walk home.

"You can't do that, Catherine. It's five miles away and you're drunk"

"I'm not drunk."

"You just told me you were drunk."

"I didn't say that."

"Oh yes you did. I'll give you a ride home, but first just open your jacket so I can check for weapons." Catherine started to take the jacket off, but Officer Rukstad told her not to, just to open it up. Under the street light, in view of passers-by, she lifted the skirts of her jacket for a moment, and then went without protest through the door Rukstad opened for her. The smell of stale cigarette smoke filled the car. Rukstad turned off his light bar.

Throughout the ride, the two bickered mildly. At one point Catherine rolled down her window and lit a cigarette.

This got a rise out of Rukstad: "Put that out! Right now! Throw it out of the car! You know better than that!"

"I'll put it out, but I won't throw it out," she said, stubbing the cigarette on the outside of the door, examining it, and then dropping it on the street.

"Jesus! It'll smell like smoke in here all night," Rukstad told me. I felt like a guest trapped in a family quarrel.

"How was I supposed to know?" Catherine asked. "You didn't tell me."

"You've been in enough police cars to know better, Catherine."

This quieted her for a few seconds, but she was ready to play whatever cards she had. "You didn't strap me in. You're supposed to strap me in."

"I'm not required to strap you in. There's a seat belt back there. Use it if you like. I'd *advise* you to use it."

By now we were on Catherine's side of town, and she decided that she didn't want to go home. She needed to go to the Sonic a few blocks from her house to work her shift, she said. And she could get something to eat there. She was hungry.

"No, Catherine. You're not going to work drunk. I'm taking you home or I'm taking you to jail and putting you in protective custody."

We were in Catherine's neighborhood now, and she pled with Officer Rukstad not to drive up to her house in his patrol car, to let her off, instead, at the foot of her street. He agreed, and as we pulled up, he told her, "I've got you home now. What you do from this point is up to you. If I were you, I believe I'd get something to eat and stay home."

Catherine didn't thank him as she got out of the car, but she shut the door gently. "What I like about this job," Officer Rukstad told me, "is that it's like a soap opera. Really, it is a soap opera."

RUKSTAD CRUISED once through his assigned beat, a quiet slice of Columbia's southwestern suburbs. For a few minutes we gazed at lawns and streetlights. Then we returned downtown, trolling down Broadway, where a crowd was milling outside a popular student bar. We turned north on Providence, where we pulled over a large pickup that had failed to signal a right turn. The computer held no reports on the middle-aged driver, who apologized and received a warning. Rukstad explained to me the strategic function of traffic stops. "When people are locked away in their cars, you can't see them. You don't know who they are or what they're doing. A stop allows you talk with them, look into their eyes, look into their vehicle."

Downtown, on a block where commercial property mixed with untidy rental houses, we fell in behind a little sedan that had seen better days. The trunk was slightly awry and there was a hole where the lock had been. There was also a chip the size of a dime missing from the cover of the right taillight—cause enough for a stop. Officer Rukstad flipped on his light bar and the sedan pulled over.

Each traffic stop followed the same pattern. Rukstad pulled up behind the citizen's car, swung the nose of his cruiser slightly into the traffic lane to shunt passing cars toward the center line, and called Joint Communications to give the number on the license plate, the nearest address, and the reason for the stop. Joint Communications would let him know if the plate was connected with a dangerous character—in this case it wasn't—and also whether the address had been associated with criminal activity—in this case it had. My training with Sergeant Smith had had its effect. Whenever Rukstad approached a car, I watched the back-up lights.

This time Rukstad returned with two driver's licenses in his hand, both from women about twenty, a black driver and a white passenger. "I recognize the driver," he told me. "She was on my old beat. Dealing in crack. Well, her brother was the crack dealer. I'm not sure about her." He ran the check on the licenses. The record on the driver was long: about thirty police reports, six or seven arrests, some for possession, none for trafficking. The passenger's record was similar but longer, about forty reports and ten arrests, including a revoked license.

Officer Rukstad called for a K-9 unit, and one pulled into a nearby parking lot within minutes. The driver of the sedan eyed the K-9 car nervously and told Rukstad that she was scared of the dog. Rukstad told the women they would be safe enough if they rolled up their windows and sat very still.

I recognized the K-9 team. The human was Todd Alber, a speaker at the Citizens' Academy. Alber had the kind of body you might see on the cover of a body-building magazine. His chest and arms filled his shirt completely; his muscles filled his skin completely. If he flexed them, something would stretch or rip. His partner was Cosmo, a German shepherd imported from Europe, where he had been carefully bred for his predatory instincts. The two had met on a farm in southeast Missouri. On the first day, under the eye of a master trainer, they had played fetch with a section of PVC pipe. Gradually, they added other games. Fetch the pipe with marijuana in it, with cocaine, with amphetamine, with heroin. Find the drug cache and dig it out of the ground or out of the wall. Bite the stranger's arm and hold it. Drag away the stranger who has Officer Alber pinned to the ground. Track the stranger across open terrain, bite and hold him. Cosmo lived for these games, which always ended in his winning the PVC pipe.

Alber had volunteered for K-9 duty because he loved dogs. ("He was so *cute!*" he told the Citizens, describing a drug-sniffing cocker spaniel he had once seen.) But that was not the only reason. When Alber was in high school, his brother—a tough kid who ran with a tough crowd—was arrested often. Sometimes he was taken to the city jail and beaten: black eyes, bruises, cuts, cracked ribs. Alber had become a cop partly because he wanted to keep that from happening to someone else's brother. He had become a K-9 officer because he knew that police dogs had been turned loose on people in America, inflicting some extra-legal punishment before lawyers and courts intervened. If a dog was coming to Columbia, he wanted to keep a firm grip on the other end of the leash.

Though Cosmo was leashed to Alber when he sprang from the back door of the K-9 car, he didn't behave like the valedictorian of an obedience school class. Head up and tail wagging, he pulled in several directions before Alber mus-cled him toward the sedan and pinned him against the trunk with one knee. I could just make out the women's outlines at that moment; short, thin girls sitting very still. Cosmo sniffed the trunk briefly and looked away. Officer Alber took him once around the car counterclockwise, once clockwise, pressing him against the metal with a knee or thigh. Cosmo seemed to be distracted; he sniffed the air in all directions. Handing the leash to Rukstad, Alber jogged back to his car and returned with the length of PVC pipe. Cosmo erupted, barking and dancing at the end of his leash as Officer Alber pretended to hide the pipe somewhere around the sedan. Alber took the leash again. On the counterclockwise pass, the dog was all business. On the clockwise pass, though, his head came up and his tail started wagging. If there were drugs in the car, Cosmo's highly trained nose wasn't focusing on them.

Officer Rukstad wrote out a warning for the taillight and let the women go. He and Alber had a tête-à-tête just out of earshot while I sat alone in the car and wondered whether this was a stop Captain Schwartze would have congratulated them for. Cosmo made a beeline for the house that had been associated with criminal activity. He sniffed the shrubbery intently for a few seconds, then cocked his leg and pissed on it. "A cat," Jeff Rukstad explained, as he got back into the cruiser.

THE COLUMBIA Police Department was choosy about its officers, we learned in our next classroom session. Applicants needed to have at least 60 hours of college credit, preferably in law enforcement studies. They had to score 70% or better on a standardized test offered by the International Police Management Association. They had to submit a handwritten essay explaining what in their background and experience fitted them for the work. They were interviewed by a panel of active officers from every rank—

patrolman to captain. If they passed through these preliminary screens, they made it onto the Eligibility Roster, along
with dozens of other applicants for the next available position.

Being on the Eligibility Roster made them the business
of Sergeant Ken Gregory, who was explaining these proce-
dures to the assembled Citizens. Gregory was a short black
man nearing fifty, bespectacled, kindly, and careful of his
words. On television he could have been cast as a doctor or
a minister. He had been reluctant to cast himself as a
policeman: "A friend of mine who was on the force kept
telling me I'd make a good officer and I should apply. I resisted. I had a good job: I didn't need this. He kept insisting
that this was the job for me. I decided to look into it."

He had worked narcotics; he was still on the SWAT
team; no doubt he knew how to rip a pistol out of the hands
of an assailant. Chiefly, though, he had signed on to prevent
crime, to be an agent of good order. He was by disposition a
Peeler.

He had been one of the first members of Columbia's
"fourth squad," an inner-city unit that also included an
idealistic young officer named Zim Schwartze. Members of
the squad got out of their patrol cars and walked their beats,
chatting with the citizens they met. They attended meetings
of the neighborhood association, shot baskets with teenagers, carved pumpkins at a block party, and hosted a fish
fry. They were invited to Christmas and Kwanzaa celebra-
tions; they invited people to ride along in their squad cars.
They helped residents pressure landlords into evicting drug
dealers and then helped the landlords manage the evictions.

"The officers," one woman told a newspaper reporter, "encourage us just by their presence."

Gregory had loved working with the fourth squad, but after it was disbanded, he left the streets and took a desk job in the personnel office. At first, it disappointed me that an officer with his good qualities—even one entering middle age—would accept such an assignment. Gradually, I began to see matters differently.

Sergeant Gregory made the Eligibility Roster, a gray patch of bureaucratic real estate, his beat. He phoned the people each applicant on the Roster had named as references. He invited them to talk candidly about the qualities that might make the applicant a good or bad officer. But, as he told us, "referees in a law-suit-happy society tend to be guarded." So he asked each of the referees for a list of additional names the candidate *hadn't* listed: neighbors and co-workers. He cold-called these people, explained how important it is that a person and a job be suited to each other, and asked them if they had any thoughts on the rightness of the applicant for police work.

He was a warm man, a good listener. Something about him invited trust and candor. When he ended a conversation, he told the person on the other end that if anything came to mind later, they should call him, any time of day or night: "I sleep with my pager in my pillow."

If candidates seemed promising, Gregory talked with them repeatedly by phone or in person. He called them on different days of the week, at different times of day, hoping to catch them at bad moments as well as good ones. He wanted to know who they really were, whether they had good senses of humor or bad tempers. He wanted to know whether they had a "run and gun" view of law enforcement. If they hadn't done police work before, he had warnings for them. "It's hard on marriages," he said, "hard on families." It's shift work; it's stressful; it exposes you to scenes of domestic violence and child abuse, "things you don't want to talk about at home."

Sergeant Gregory spent as much time discouraging people from becoming police offers as he did recruiting them. He cared about the people he was talking with. He didn't want them to make a mistake with their lives. Above all, he didn't want his community to be saddled with a bad cop.

EMOTIONALLY, THE most difficult session of the Academy was one with three announced topics: the domestic violence squad, the narcotics squad, and a "guest speaker." For more than an hour, we heard about women beaten, cut, burned, and killed by the men they lived with. We saw pictures of swollen faces and bruises in various stages of maturity. I can't make myself remember these photos in detail, but I do remember the photograph of a padlock on the outside of a door of a house in my hometown, a padlock intended to keep a woman from escaping. I remember the officers' description of relationships in which one person ("usually but not always a man") utterly controls and humiliates another.

That presentation nearly did me in, and it was a relief to move on to the narcotics officer, who clearly loved his job—loved outwitting the bad guys, loved adopting new disguises and identities and working undercover. He loved, though he wouldn't quite say it, the danger and the glamour of the work, and he was confident that he was doing the right thing.

By the time he finished, we were nearly three hours into the class and, frankly, I hoped we would skip the guest speaker. But there she was, a blonde woman, "S," introduced by her own name and ready to talk. And talk. The narcotics man, who had started for the door, turned around and found a seat at the back of the room.

She was a pretty woman, about thirty years old, with a complexion that suggested good health, but she was also a bundle of neurotic tics. As she spoke, she tossed her head. Periodically, her right hand would claw at her left arm, then her left hand would claw at her right arm. She was, she told us, a drug addict, though straight for a year now, and she believed what people told her about drug addicts being people born with addictive personalities. From the time she was young, she couldn't do anything in moderation. Potato chips, Diet Coke, men—oh, she loved men—everything to excess.

She had graduated from high school in Columbia. She had smoked marijuana steadily for ten years and functioned well enough in the world, but then her boyfriend tricked her into smoking crack cocaine, "and that was it, I knew from the first hit that nothing else would matter." She couldn't keep a job; she couldn't keep the baby she gave up for adoption; she moved to St. Louis with her boyfriend. When they were both arrested for possession, his family hired a pricey lawyer who got the charges against him dismissed. She used a court-appointed lawyer and was sentenced to the first of several treatment programs she failed to complete.

Her lawyer was a heavy drug user himself, and quite well off. For several months, he kept her supplied with crack on fairly easy terms ("Always take money for sex if you can, then pay for your own drugs. It gives you a measure of control"). The easy supply was catastrophic. "S" woke up alone one morning on the floor of an abandoned building in a part of St. Louis she would never walk through in broad daylight. She was down to ninety pounds. Clearly, she was going to die. Her sister intervened and brought her to Columbia, where she would be safe.

The difficulty was that "S" was still addicted to crack and could no longer get it from a relatively safe source. In Columbia, she had to deal directly with serious criminals, offering what services she could in return. She shoplifted often from the mall. "The guy would give me a regular shopping list: this kind of dress, this size, shoes to match. And, frankly," she added with a sad smile, "I sucked a lot of dick." I looked around the conference table at this point to see how the Citizens were reacting. There were several absolutely frozen smiles.

At one point, she was kidnapped, taken out of town and kept prisoner for three days. Once again, she knew that she was headed toward death. She had another child, and she desperately wanted to stay alive to raise him. She tried holding down a job as a waitress, tried to stay straight, but she couldn't do it alone. Her family was frightened and confused. Her boyfriend wanted her to keep doing drugs with him. She was bounced out of a treatment program because she was caught "fraternizing" with one of the men in her group. She was boxed in.

One night she was waiting tables at Sirloin Stockade when a customer, a middle-aged black man, neatly dressed, walked up to her and said quietly, "If you need some help, call me, any time of day or night." He handed her a card. "S" was puzzled. "I don't know what he saw in me that told him I wanted help," she told us Citizens, her fingernails motionless for a moment in the red tracks they had made along her arms. She kept the card beside her bed and thought about it for a few days:

> Sergeant Kenneth Gregory
> Columbia Police Department

Eventually, she called.

Jury Duty

There was no final exam in the Citizens' Academy. I received a diploma, wrote up my notes, put them in a drawer, and left them there for seven years. During those seven years, I didn't talk to anyone I knew to be either a policeman or a criminal—unless we count reefer-smoking college professors and tax-evading business owners.

I kept up with police matters through the newspapers. Early in 2005, I read about the death of Molly Bowden, a young officer who was patrolling a suburban beat alone at night when she made a routine traffic stop. She approached the car and asked the driver for his license. He was a white college student, twenty-three years old, three years younger than Bowden. A video taken from the camera mounted in her cruiser shows that Bowden and the man talked for thirty-nine seconds before he murdered her with a .38-caliber pistol. The next day he wounded another officer and then killed himself.

Columbia is a small city with a police force of fewer than 150 officers. Molly Bowden was the first one to be killed in the line of duty. I suspect that after Bowden's death, officers became less enthusiastic about community-oriented policing. Getting out of a patrol car in a high-crime area to chat with the residents can't have seemed as appealing as it once did. In 2009, the police chief retired. Captain Schwartze applied for the job and didn't get so much as an interview. This was, she told a reporter, "disappointing." She took a leave from her duties in the department and became interim director of the city's 911 center.

EARLY IN the spring of 2010, I sat on a jury for the first time. After a morning spent in jury selection, the trial began with the judge letting us know that the charge was "failure to obey a lawful police order." We were to evaluate the evidence in the case, she said, in light of our "common sense" and "life experience." I thought back on the Citizens' Academy and realized that there might be a final exam, after all.

The smiling prosecutor rose to wish us good morning and deliver his opening statement. He told us that this trial was entirely about the defendant's bad choices, which had escalated what might have been a routine traffic stop into a crisis. He also told us that the defendant and his attorney were cooking up a lawsuit against the police department, and that an acquittal on this criminal charge would increase their chances of winning a hefty cash judgment. The defense objected strenuously to the speculation about the supposed lawsuit. The judge sustained the objection. She asked us to ignore the comment, which fixed it firmly in our memory.

The defense attorney rose in turn and said that the trial was really about out-of-control policemen violating the rights of an innocent citizen. He said the beating his client had taken had made him personally very angry. He grimaced fiercely. He was dressed in a conservative vested suit and a pink shirt. The shirt would be much commented on during the jury's deliberations, often with a smile and a wag of the head: "… and that shirt he wore!"

The central piece of evidence in the case was a video of a traffic stop as recorded by a camera mounted in a police car. As the day progressed, a cloud of testimony began to crystallize around this video.

On the Video/…/*On the Witness Stand*

It is about 3:00 p.m. on a mild February day. The camera shows a Subaru wagon signaling a left turn onto four-lane Providence Road. As the Subaru turns, the police car in which we seem to be sitting turns behind it and the light bar comes on. The Subaru pulls into the right-hand lane, passes one side street, and pulls to the curb. We hear Officer Hogan* say, "What the hell, dude!" as he stops behind the Subaru.

> *Officer Hogan testifies that he pulled the car over because he had earlier passed it nose-to-nose and noticed that it didn't have a front license plate. He had turned his car around to get behind the Subaru.*
>
> *He explains "What the hell, dude!" as an expression of surprise: he had expected the driver to pull onto the side street, where there was less danger to everyone from passing traffic.*

---

* I use pseudonyms for all parties involved in the case. Serious researchers will have no difficulty finding the actual names of the officers and the defendant in the public record.

We hear a voice booming from the cruiser's outside mega-
phone, but the words are unclear. The Subaru doesn't move.
Officer Eiger, a burly, uniformed white man in his late thirties, gets out of the cruiser's passenger seat and walks the
few steps to the Subaru's passenger-side door. He talks to
the occupants and points down the road. We hear Hogan
radioing in the plate number of the Subaru.

> *Officer Eiger testifies that when he approached the
> Subaru, he told the occupants to pull onto the next side
> street. Both the defendant, Mercury Merrick, and his
> girlfriend, Amanda Ross, explain that they decided to
> drive past the side street, which was lined by apartment
> buildings, and to stop in the strip mall. They were
> frightened by police officers, they say, and thought they
> would be safer in a more visible, public place.*

The Subaru starts slowly forward, passing a side street on
the right and pulling into the parking lot of a small strip
mall, nose facing the plate-glass front of a payday loan
office. For a few seconds there is no motion except the
flashing of the light from the light bar.

> *Testimony from several witnesses shows that the car
> was jointly registered to Merrick and Ross, and that
> each had a prior conviction: he for assault and she for
> possession of marijuana. Merrick says that his convic-
> tion had come five years earlier, when he was 17 and
> got into a fight with a friend. He was, he acknowledges,
> tried as an adult. Ross says that her conviction for pos-
> session came six years earlier, when she was 17. She
> stopped using marijuana, she says, "five or six years*

ago," after she learned that she was pregnant, and has not used it since.

Officer Hogan, a uniformed white man in his early thirties, approaches the driver's side door and speaks rapidly. "How're you doing today, I need to see your license and insurance." Merrick's hand comes almost immediately out of the window, handing over the documents. By now Officer Eiger is at the Subaru's passenger-side door. Officer Hogan glances at the driver's license and the insurance documents. As he does, we hear Merrick ask, "Why are you stopping me?" "Because you don't have a license," Hogan replies.

"I misspoke. I should have said 'front license plate,'" Officer Hogan explains with a shrug.

Hogan looks across the top of the Subaru at Eiger and slides a finger along one side of his nose. Eiger lowers his face to the window of the opposite door, raises it again, looks at Hogan, and shakes his head no.

Hogan explains that the finger along the nose was a signal meaning, "I smell drugs." He says that when he sent the signal, Eiger "nodded." Eiger says he didn't smell marijuana at that moment, but that he smelled it later.

Officer Hogan says, "I need you to step out of the car." Merrick doesn't respond. Twice Merrick asks, "Can I have my ID back?" Officer Hogan doesn't respond either time. In a voice that shows irritation or agitation, Merrick says, "I'm not getting out."

Merrick says that six months earlier officers had stopped him, said they had a warrant for his arrest, and taken him to the station, where it was discovered that the warrant was issued for someone else. He was released. Police hadn't beaten him, he admits on cross-examination, but they hadn't offered him a ride home, either. "I had to walk home." Eiger testifies that he had been one of the arresting officers on that occasion, and that he had found Merrick polite and cooperative.

Hogan opens the door and says firmly, "You're getting out." He grasps Merrick's left arm with his right hand. Merrick leans to his right, getting as far from Hogan as possible. Hogan reaches deep into the car with his left hand, apparently attempting to grab Merrick by both shoulders. From our point of view, we can see that Eiger is at the passenger-side window, but cannot see what he has in his right hand.

Eiger says that he was frightened. "The suspect is moving toward the center console of the car. This is where people keep guns. I see my partner being pulled into the car. The pistol in his holster is exposed now. The adrenaline is flowing; it's fight-or-flight kicking in. I have mace, but the girl is between me and the suspect. I can't use it without hitting her. I can't use pepper spray with the child in the back seat. So I use the taser." He explains that because both taser probes struck Merrick in the upper arm, only inches apart, the electric current running between them caused pain, but didn't immobilize whole muscle groups. Realizing this, Eiger attempted to touch Merrick with the taser gun itself, creating a longer circuit, but he couldn't reach him.

Merrick flies out of the car, screaming. He falls to the pavement, screaming, leaps up and runs, still screaming. We see Officer Hogan grab his coat as he passes. The coat comes off. Merrick and the two officers run out of the picture frame. For about 15 minutes the video shows us only the reactions of bystanders. Ross, a white woman in her early twenties, jumps out of the passenger seat of the Subaru and waves her arms, yelling words we can't understand. She goes briefly into the payday loan office, walks out again, leaves the frame, returns talking excitedly into a cell phone, drifts out of sight once more. In the back seat her daughter gradually works herself free of her seatbelt and whatever other restraint she may have been in. She peers out of the back window. Someone looks out the door of the loan office; someone else comes out of the storefront next door and snaps pictures. Through the microphone on Officer Hogan's lapel, we can hear the muffled sounds of a struggle. Merrick continues to scream constantly. At one point we can understand a few of his words: "They're killing me!" Eventually the screaming and the sounds of the struggle subside.

The officers testify that they were able to catch Merrick because he tripped over a curb and fell face down. They threw themselves on top of him and dug fingertips into the "pressure points" on his face and neck, attempting to control him with pain. When this didn't work, they tried to immobilize his arms and legs by striking them repeatedly at key nerve bundles. They used open hands and closed fists. When this didn't work, they used repeated knee kicks to the legs and arms. Eiger says that he asked Hogan to use his taser. Hogan explains he was unable to do this because the battery was malfunctioning. Instead, Eiger wrapped an arm around Merrick's neck and squeezed it, applying a "lateral vascular neck restraint" designed to cut off blood flow to the brain and render the suspect unconscious. "It may look like strangling," Hogan explains, "but it isn't. The windpipe is protected by the crook of the elbow." Ross says that during the struggle, she called 911 for help.

Eiger explains that other officers, "five or six," soon appeared at the scene to help. "Two or three" threw themselves onto the struggling Merrick. Eiger says that even in a prone position with his hands above his head and officers on his shoulders, Merrick was strong enough to push his face and upper body off the concrete. Merrick says that he heard the officers tell him to put his hands behind his back and that he attempted to do so, but couldn't because the officers had his arms pinned above his head ("like this," he demonstrates).

Ross opens a car door to let her daughter out. For the rest of the video, the girl stays by her mother's side, following her every move. Several officers, including one sergeant, search the Subaru's passenger compartment, looking for weapons or drugs. They open the trunk and search it, too, discovering four blankets and a gallon of antifreeze. The search lasts for about ten minutes. Officer Hogan is especially thorough.

We see him going through coat pockets and turning the fingers of a pair of gloves inside out.

Officers Hogan and Eiger and their sergeant acknowledge that no drugs or drug paraphernalia were found. Neither were any weapons found, unless we count two closed pocket knives lying on pavement near the car.

Ross is screaming at the officers: "I'm going to sue your butts! I'm going to sue all your butts! I want names! I want all your names!" Officer Hogan doesn't hide his irritation. He tells her that she needs "to put that kid in a child restraint." Otherwise, he says, he will cite her for child endangerment. He has a pad in his hand and seems to be writing a citation. The sergeant pulls out his wallet and hands the woman his business card. "We're going to give her everything she needs," he says. The video ends.

Officer Eiger says that he is unable to recall whether there was a child seat in the back of the car.

THE TESTIMONY ended at about 3:30 and we were sent without explanation to the jury room. I knew enough about legal procedure to suggest to a confused fellow juror that the lawyers were now going to argue about what the judge's final instructions would be. I didn't say—because we had been instructed not to discuss the case in any way—that I was *hungry* for the instructions. I had no opinion at that moment about whether Merrick was guilty or innocent. A crime, I knew, had elements that the prosecution needed to prove beyond a reasonable doubt. Until someone revealed the elements, I was clueless.

The negotiation over jury instructions must have been complicated: we waited for most of an hour. We talked about the role of cell phones and Facebook in the lives of the rising generation, a half-hearted conversation that had filled parts of every break. In general, I was inclined to think well of my fellow jurors, who seemed to be paying close attention to the testimony, and who had scrupulously followed the judge's instructions about not discussing the case until final instructions were given.

After the conversation about Facebook faded, a young man I'll call Tom* filled a few awkward minutes by telling stories about his hunting dogs. Then the room went silent. Lana, a schoolteacher who was perhaps the cleverest person in the room, laughed and observed that we could only spend so many hours talking about nothing. We sat alone with our thoughts for perhaps fifteen more minutes before we were called back.

The judge issued several instructions that were essentially rules of the road. That the defendant was presumed innocent until proven guilty; that the fact of being charged was not evidence of guilt; that we were to consult our common sense and life experience in evaluating evidence; that the prosecution must prove all elements of the alleged crime beyond a reasonable doubt. And then at last, she gave the elements:

---

* Like the principals in the case, the jurors have been assigned pseudonyms.

1. On or about February 24, 2009, Officer Hogan was ·employed as a police officer in Columbia, Missouri. AND

2. On or about February 24, 2009, Officer Hogan attempted to detain the defendant. AND

3. The defendant reasonably should have understood that Officer Hogan was acting in his capacity as a police officer when he attempted the detention. AND

4. The basis of the detention was the smell of marijuana in the defendant's vehicle. AND

5. The defendant reasonably should have understood the basis of the detention. AND

6. The defendant resisted the officer's attempt to detain him.

Ordinarily, my mind moves slowly, but in this case it leapt. There could be no reasonable doubt about elements one through three. There could be doubt about four and possibly six. I might have worried about whether the doubt was strong enough to be reasonable, but I didn't need to because element five clearly had *not* been demonstrated. Officer Hogan had told Merrick (erroneously) that the basis of the detention was driving without a license. Why would Merrick think that the basis of the detention was actually the smell of marijuana in the vehicle? I listened closely to the closing arguments of both attorneys without hearing anything that changed my mind.

We returned to the jury room, relieved to be able to talk about the case and, I think, uniformly convinced that we would reach a verdict quickly. We elected as foreman the woman who happened to be sitting next to the door. She suggested that we begin with a test vote, and we agreed. She asked how many at this point were inclined to vote guilty. Eleven hands went up.

I TOLD my fellow jurors that I found being alone on the other side socially awkward, but that I felt it was my duty to vote not guilty. Several expressed sympathy and encouragement. I explained that my problem was chiefly with the fifth element in the instructions, which seemed to say that the defendant couldn't be found guilty unless he knew, or should have known, that the officer was detaining him because of the smell of marijuana. I said I doubted he knew this. A juror about seventy years old, whom I will call Fran, said she didn't know what I was talking about when I said the fifth element. She reminded me that the judge had said we were supposed to use our *common sense*. Merrick was charged with resisting arrest, she said. We had *seen* him resisting arrest on the video. *Common sense* told us he was guilty.

The foreman thought it might be useful to go through the instructions one element at a time. We had only one copy of the instructions, so she read them aloud. All of us agreed that the first three elements had been proven. When we got to element four, Lana commented that she had *some* doubt that the smell of marijuana was the cause of the detention. She wasn't entirely sure that she believed Officer Hogan's statement that he had smelled it. She said, however, that this was a *small* doubt.

I said I also had a small doubt here. When Hogan submitted the Subaru's license number, he could have seen on his computer screen a note about Ross's prior arrest for possession. That would have given him reason to want to search the car. On the video, Hogan's rubbing his nose looked more like a question—"Do you smell dope?"—than a statement. And Eiger had clearly shaken his head "no." It bothered me that Hogan had testified that Eiger had nodded "yes." Perhaps there had never been a marijuana smell. Perhaps Hogan had invented the smell after the fact to defend his aggressive policing. But, I said, I might be able to set that doubt aside. As I talked, Fran grimaced and shifted in her chair. "Oh, come *on*!" she said now. "Stop inventing this stuff. The judge said we didn't have to deal with every possible doubt. Use your *common sense*."

We moved on to element five. I pointed out that element four had indicated clearly that "the basis of the detention" had to be the "smell of marijuana." And so when element five said that Merrick had to understand the "basis of the detention," it must mean that he had to understand he was being detained because one or both officers smelled marijuana. But Hogan had told Merrick that he was being detained for driving without a license. Merrick was not a mind reader. I didn't see how we could "reasonably" expect him to understand that the real basis for the detention was anything other than what Hogan had told him. No one's eyes actually rolled as I explained this, but I had been a teacher for more than twenty-five years, and I recognized that some of the other jurors wished I would just stop talking.

Fran said, "Well, if all that is true, why didn't Merrick's lawyer say anything about it? Why are you arguing for him?"

At this point a woman I'll call Holly jumped in. "Look," she said. "Marijuana has a very strong smell, a very distinctive smell. I should know; I smoked plenty when I was a kid, and I spent a lot of time spraying myself with perfume so people wouldn't catch me. If Merrick was smoking dope, he knew he smelled like dope; every smoker does. Officer Hogan didn't have to tell Merrick that he was arresting him because he smelled like marijuana. He understood what he was being arrested for. You smoke dope, you risk arrest, and you know it."

But, I said, Officer Eiger sniffed at the other door and didn't smell marijuana. Merrick can't have reeked of the stuff. "Oh yes he could have," said Tom, the hunting-dog man, who also seemed very knowledgeable about marijuana. "Eiger was sniffing at the passenger-side door. I bet he couldn't smell it on that side because the girl was smart enough to roll down her window. They kept driving for two or three blocks so fresh air would come in the window. They were smokers; they knew the score. They kept driving while she aired out the car and threw away the joint."

Back and forth we went for more than an hour. The foreman asked if we should vote again. We did. This time it was 8 guilty, 4 innocent. The bailiff knocked at the door and asked if we wanted to send out for supper. We decided we'd better do so, and—at Holly's suggestion—we sent out for the video and a laptop to view it with.

The three other "not guilties" were Lana (the schoolteacher), George (a middle-aged black man), and Bill (a middle-aged white man). Lana began to waver about 7:30. She looked at the instruction sheet and said, "I don't think that item four and item five are that closely related. There is an *and* between them, but there are *and*s between all the items. If items four and five aren't definitely linked, then the 'basis of the detention' in item four might be different from the 'basis of the detention' in item five."

Holly agreed enthusiastically. The "basis of the detention," she said, probably shifted several times in the course of the arrest. Maybe it started as a detention over a missing license plate, and then became a detention over marijuana, and then a detention for resisting arrest. Merrick may not have known the basis of all these detentions, but by the end, he had to understand he had been detained for resisting arrest.

I said that this argument seemed circular. He resisted arrest, and that's why he was being arrested? That made no sense to me. Fran snorted. "Come *on!*" she scolded me, shaking her head.

Bill asked to see the instruction sheet. He studied it. "No. I don't see how the 'basis of the detention' can mean one thing in one sentence and something entirely different in the next. The words are the same." We decided to send an inquiry to the judge: "To find the defendant guilty, must we conclude beyond a reasonable doubt that he should reasonably have understood the basis of the detention to be the smell of marijuana?" The judge's answer came back within five minutes. "Read the instructions." We groaned.

We played the video again, on the chance that it would somehow help us. Fran watched Ross leap out of the car and start talking on the phone. "Look at her," she said. "What kind of mother is she? She leaves her daughter all alone in that back seat. The first thing a good mother would do is make sure that child is safe."

"Well," Lana observed mildly, "there are plenty of policemen around, so the kid probably wasn't in much danger."

We watch Ross go into the payday loan office briefly and come back out. "That's probably where she got rid of the evidence, right there," Tom said.

"I'll bet you're right," said Holly. "The police didn't search the store."

"And she says she's calling 911, as if she wanted was more policemen on the scene," said Fran. "This is a set-up. They are trying to trap the police and sue them. That's why they wouldn't pull off on a side street. They wanted witnesses for their little act. What are they doing driving around at 3:00 in the afternoon? They don't have jobs; you can bet on that. They have to find some way to make money, and they think this is it. Use your common sense, why would she call 911?"

"You bet," Tom said. "It's all an act. They planned this out in advance."

"I think I might have called 911," Lana said.

The foreman and I watched the early minutes of the video again. I noticed this time that the Subaru's passenger-side window was definitely up when Merrick turned into the strip mall. I considered pointing this out to Tom, as a challenge to his airing-out-the-car theory, but decided it would only antagonize him. Positions had hardened now. People were especially tired of hearing me talk. We might snipe at each other, but we weren't likely to change any minds.

Bill didn't watch the video again. He sat very still, considering whether Merrick understood that he was being detained because his car smelled like marijuana. At this point, he crossed a threshold. He looked across the table at me and said, "If the car didn't smell like marijuana, why did he act the way he acted? Answer me that."

I was tempted to say that Merrick was a young black man who may have grown up hearing stories of police violence, and that he might have been reluctant to leave the safety of a car parked in a public view and give himself over to an aggressive officer like Hogan. I found, though, that I was reluctant to mention race directly in a room already gone fractious. I responded weakly. "I don't know, and I don't have to know. Perhaps because he had already had unpleasant encounters with the police."

"The police treated him well when they arrested him before," Holly said. "They didn't hurt him. He had no reason to be afraid." It was after 9:00. We had been in the jury room for four hours. At this point the foreman suggested that we might vote again. I asked for a few minutes to think. Without support from Bill and Lana, I was beginning to doubt my doubts. Emotionally, I am ashamed to say, I was ready to go over to the other side, to show everyone that I had common sense, too. But, no, I couldn't convince myself to let go of the fifth element. I believed in the system enough to assume that it was in the instructions for a good reason. If a citizen couldn't understand why he was being detained, was it a crime for him to sit still and not step out of the car? Why was the charge "failure to obey a *lawful* police order" if the citizen had automatically to consider every police order lawful?

We voted. This time it was 10 to convict; 2 to acquit. "I think we are a hung jury," I told the foreman.

She thought it might be useful if George, who had said almost nothing all day, explained why he was voting not guilty. George cleared his throat. "It makes a lot of difference to me that they didn't find any marijuana in the car. I don't see any evidence that these people were smoking."

Holly reminded him that we had been told that testimony is evidence, and that Officer Hogan testified that he smelled marijuana. "Policemen sometimes lie," George replied. "Doctors lie. Even ministers lie. They're only human." He pointed out that Eiger said he didn't smell marijuana.

"*At the time*," Holly said. "He said he smelled it later."

"Policemen cover up for their partners. There is loyalty among them. There was no marijuana in the car."

"Look," Holly said, "you don't have to have physical evidence to know that people are drug users. Sometimes you can tell by just looking at them, sometimes you can tell by the smell."

George erupted. "So you can just *look* at some people and *know* they are guilty, can you?" Now, clearly, we were talking about race. "Nothing in this case makes sense to me. It just doesn't add up. They didn't find marijuana in the car. Nothing you can say will ever convince me to vote guilty because there is no physical proof."

"Well," said Fran, "if you weren't willing to consider all the evidence, you should have said so before you were picked for the jury."

Just before 10:00, we filed back into the courtroom. I half-expected to find it empty and dark, but all the lawyers were there, the court reporter, Merrick, and two bailiffs. Six people were still sitting in the gallery: Ross and her daughter, two men who seemed to be there to offer Merrick their moral support, and—far to the rear—officers Hogan and Eiger. I didn't want to meet anyone's eye. The foreman announced that we were unable to reach a verdict. The judge asked her if additional time might allow us to break our deadlock. If so, she could make arrangements for us to continue the next day. The foreman said no. The judge declared a mistrial and thanked us with apparent sincerity for our service. "Don't feel that your time has been wasted. Without the participation of citizens like you, our system of justice could not function." She said that, "in light of the hour" the bailiffs would accompany us out of the courthouse and across the street and would watch to see that we reached our cars safely.

We walked down the marble stairs past the mural showing scenes of Boone County's judicial past. The first meeting of the circuit court, where there was a dispute over a wolf's scalp; the quelling of a lynch mob by a silver-bearded lawyer; the erection of the earlier courthouse with its cryptic motto on the lintel: "Oh, Justice, when expelled from other habitations, make this thy dwelling place." In a few minutes, the bailiffs joined us. They carried two-way radios and had their weapons strapped to their belts. Thus escorted, we crossed the street safely.

I hadn't driven to the courthouse, so when the bailiffs and the other jurors entered the parking garage, I skirted it and walked west down Broadway. It was a mild St. Patrick's Day, so I expected to see a crowd milling outside McNally's pub, but the sidewalks were nearly empty. It was the middle of the week, I realized, and early yet for serious drinkers. As I waited for the light to change at an intersection, a couple of young men caught up with me, one of them slightly unsteady on his legs. They weren't talking about crime; they were talking about basketball. A squad car passed slowly. Having spent the whole day immersed in the police officers' world, I felt a fleeting impulse to wave, but common sense won out. I kept my hands in my pockets and concentrated on looking innocent.

Notes and Sources

Acknowledgements

I owe special thanks to Bill Stolz and Mary Beth Brown, who helped me in more ways than I can count during their tenure at the Western Historical Manuscript Collection and afterward. Thanks also to several colleagues and friends who have repeatedly edited, proofread, advised and encouraged, notably Marj Hunt, Peter Hessler, Bill Dawson, George Justice, John Estes, and Abby Jaskolski.

Names

Much of the general information about legal cases involving slaves other than Sanford Shirkey comes from North Todd Gentry's *The Bench and Bar of Boone County Missouri* (1916). The slave Dinah is mentioned in the Records of Columbia Presbyterian Church (Western Historical Manuscripts Collection, Columbia, C2308). The interview with James Williams appeared in the Columbia *Missourian*, September 26, 1935. Additional information about the slave's status under the law is drawn from Harrison Anthony Trexler's *Slavery in Missouri* (1914). On the attitudes toward their slaves of Walter and Sarah Lenoir, see Lewis E. Atherton's "Life, Labor and Society in Boone County, Missouri, 1834-1852" *Missouri Historical Review* (Volume 38, 1944).

Gentry's *Bench and Bar* provided material for sketching the characters of David and North Todd and of Peyton Hayden. Additional information on these three men was gathered from the North Todd Gentry papers (WHMC, C0049). Details of the Reavis-Shirkey feud are drawn from legal documents and transcripts are available in the Missouri State Archives (Boone Circuit Court case of *Sanford versus Reavis*, and Saline Circuit Court joined cases of *Shelby, Julia, Eliza, and Tina versus Solomon Reavis*). I owe a great debt to Barbara Lucas of Port Orange, Florida, a tenacious researcher who launched a search for these court documents and was generous enough to send me a copy. The Green County [MO Library] *Archive Bulletin*, Number 45, notes the existence of an 1834 subpoena in the case, summoning Mark Reavis from Pettus [sic] County.

See thelibrary.springfield.missouri.org for an online version of the *Bulletin*. Philip Shirkey's letter to the *Arkansas Gazette* was published August 29, 1832. See the Arkansas Ties website (www.arkansasties.com) for an online version of the letter.

Legwork by Barbara Lucas and other Reavis family genealogists (much of it posted on Ancestry.com and elsewhere on the web) helped me flesh out biographical details important to the Reavis/Shirkey story. Mark Reavis's conflict with John Sears over the slave Oney can be traced in legal documents available in the Missouri State Archives. These documents are summarized in the University of North Carolina - Greensboro's *Digital Library on American Slavery*.

See www.angelfire.com/fl3/reavisrevis for a copy of Isham Reavis's will. His deed emancipating Patience is included in the anonymously compiled *History of Saline County, Missouri* (Missouri Historical Company, 1881) as is the Reavis family story in which we learn that Mark Reavis was advised by a lawyer to sell Sant contrary to court orders. Barbara Lucas has explained to me that this story was written by Edwin Reavis, a nephew of one of Sanford's kidnappers.

The key sources for information about the great meteor shower of 1833 were two articles from *Sky and Telescope*: Richard Sanderson's "The Night of Raining Fire." (November 1998), and Donald W. Olson and Laurie E. Jasinski's "Abe Lincoln and the Leonids" (November, 1999). Also useful were John P. Pratt's "Spectacular Meteor Shower Might Repeat" in *Meridian Magazine* (October 15, 1999) and J. Campbell's "Meteoric Showers: An Eyewitness Account of the Display in November, 1833." (New York *Times*, November 9, 1879). Anne Todd (Mrs. Anne E. Campbell's) description of the shower as seen in Columbia appeared in the Columbia Missouri Herald December 21, 1900, and can be found in the North Todd Gentry papers (WHMC, C0049). Switzler's story of the meteor shower freeing Sant appeared in the Kansas City *Star*, May 7, 1904. North Todd Gentry supplements Switzler's account in an unpublished note (WHMC, C0049, folder 152).

In dealing with primary sources, I have sometimes silently amended punctuation and spelling.

A Course in Applied Lynching

The principal sources for this essay are scores of newspaper articles published from April 20 through July 25, 1923, most of them in local newspapers: the Columbia

Missourian, *Daily Tribune*, and *Herald-Statesman*; the St. Louis *Post-Dispatch*, *Globe-Democrat* and *Argus*; the Kansas City *Star* and the Mexico *Ledger*. Bibliographical information on the bulk of these can be found in Patrick J. Huber's excellent undergraduate thesis *Town vs. Gown: The James T. Scott Lynching and the Social Fracture between the University of Missouri and the Larger Columbia Community*. Huber's thesis, which I consulted on hundreds of details, is available in the State Historical Society of Missouri. It was reworked as "The Lynching of James T. Scott: The Underside of a College Town." *Gateway Heritage* 12:1 (Summer 1991).

Newspaper reports beyond the core time period also proved valuable. The *Missourian* reported earlier incidents of James Scott's life in Columbia (September 22, 1920; January 22, 1921; August 4 and 19, 1922). The St. Louis *Argus* (May 6 and 20, 1921) and Bowling Green *Times* (May 5 and 12) reported the lynching of Roy Hammond. Ruby Hulen's campaign biography appeared July 29, 1920 in the *Missourian* and the *Tribune*. His suicide was covered by the *New York Times* (July 8 and 10, 1956). George Vaughn's career is summarized in the *New York Times* (August 18, 1949) and the St. Louis *Argus* (August 19). Henry Davis's war memories appeared in *The Lead Belt News* (Flat River, MO), February 14, 1919. George Starrett's donkey baseball victory was reported in the Columbia *Daily Tribune*, July 21, 1934.

Recent redactions of the James Scott story are Bob Beasley's "Echoes from Stewart Bridge: The Last Lynching in Columbia" (Columbia *Senior Times*, September 1996), and Barton Grover Howe's five-part series in the Columbia *Missourian* (May 5-9, 2003).

Three collections in the Western Historical Manuscript Collection at the University of Missouri proved very useful. Oral histories from the Haskell Monroe Collection give a vivid sense of life in Columbia in the twenties and thirties. The Arthur Hyde Papers reveal the Governor's personality and his role in the lynching story, and also include letters from John Williams, George Vaughn, and others. Information on the Round Table club is in the Sarah Lockwood Williams Collection. Letters from Ruby Hulen are scattered through several collections at WHMC. Francis Misselwitz's account of Walter Williams' patronage can be found in the University of Missouri Archives (Roy M. Fisher Papers).

Charles Ellwood's *Introduction to Sociology* presents his views on the "group mind." Dorothy Nowell Peavey's *A Third of My Days* provides details of life in the period, including her memories of sleeping with her umbrella at the ready and of the Harrisburg's warning sign for blacks. The *Methodist Foundation Herald*, published by Joseph Randolph's church (State Historical Society of Missouri) reveals his mild theology. His son Jack's description of the lynching during a 1968 poetry class at Westminster College was the seed from which this project grew.

I am deeply indebted to Patrick Huber, Patricia Roberts (a granddaughter of Hermann Almstedt) and David Sapp (a remarkable local historian) for providing information about James T. Scott and his family, mined with great labor from many sources while we worked together on the James T. Scott memorial project of 2010-2011.

Watching the Watchers

Most of the information in the first part of this essay was drawn directly from lectures and demonstrations at the Citizen's Police Academy. Supplementary material was drawn from the Columbia *Daily Tribune* and the Columbia *Missourian*. Both covered the Ken Smith milkshake incident and the resulting lawsuit during the first three months of 1983. Both covered the Kim Linzie shooting and its aftermath in July, 1985. On Linzie, see especially the *Tribune*'s front-page stories from July 5-7 and July 14. For activities of the old "fourth squad" see articles published in the *Tribune* January 23 and 30, 1994, and December 4, 1996.

Jurors are not allowed to take notes in the courtroom, and jurors are not allowed to leave the jury room with notes taken there, so my reporting on the trial of Mercury Merrick, including the judge's instructions, is necessarily from memory.

The named parties in the Merrick case have been assigned pseudonyms, but serious researchers can easily identify them from the public record and newspapers accounts, and can, in fact, view the arrest video evidence on YouTube, where it was posted by Merrick's lawyer.

14174786R00105

Made in the USA
Lexington, KY
12 March 2012